Ken Duncan

Life's a Journey

THE ADVENTURE CONTINUES

THIS BOOK IS DEDICATED TO MY BEAUTIFUL SISTERS ANNIE AND JENNIE.
THANKS FOR ALWAYS BEING THERE FOR ME. YOUR LOVE AND SUPPORT HAS
GIVEN ME GREAT STRENGTH IN MY ADVENTURES THROUGH LIFE.

PANOGRAPHS
PUBLISHING PTY LTD

ENJOY THE JOURNEY
ENJOY THE JOURNEY

Ken

Duncan

Life's a Journey

THE ADVENTURE CONTINUES

PANOGRAPHS®
PUBLISHING PTY LTD

Sheathers Wharf, Koolewong, NSW

THOUGHT

Soon after this image was taken, the entire location changed dramatically.
Procrastination can be the greatest obstacle to fulfilling our dreams:
if we don't seize opportunities when they arise, we may miss them forever.
I often wonder how many opportunities have been lost through inactivity.

Giant Panda, Chengdu, China

Here's a little song I wrote, You might want to sing it note for note. Don't worry, be happy
In every life we have some trouble, But when you worry you make it double. Don't worry, be happy…

BOBBY McFERRIN

Special Thanks

Without support from many people and companies, it would be difficult for me to pursue my passion of photographing our beautiful world. I would like to convey my heartfelt thanks to those who have helped me along the way.

Special thanks to my great staff who can share equal pride in all we achieve as a team. Thanks to Janet Gough, my friend and co-conspirator in publishing. She is a living legend and a great motivator. Thanks to the friends I have made along my journey – you add character and colour to my life.

Mountains of love to my wonder woman wife, Pam, and my precious daughter, Jessica, for their faith in me and their unwavering support. You truly are my treasures beyond measure.

Thank you also to our wonderful clients who have been there over the years. I consider your purchases the highest compliments of my work. They help make the journey possible and keep me clicking.

I would especially like to acknowledge the following companies for their assistance in bringing this book to fruition. Each has been specially invited to join me on this project because I am passionate about the products and services they offer. They are the best in their respective fields and when you work with the best it makes the job a lot more fun.

Ken Duncan, OAM

des

My fine art prints are inkjet printed on Hahnemühle Fine Art paper with an overlaying Hahnemühle UV matt varnish. I consider this the best digital fine art paper in the world. I highly recommend DES Pty Ltd who supply Hahnemühle papers and all your other digital printing requirements from inkjet printers and inks to profiling and technical services. www.des-pl.com.au

Bellini FINE MOULDING

Framing with Bellini Fine Mouldings has taken the presentation of my fine art prints to a whole new level of elegance. Bellini say "the frame is the artist's reward". I believe it is also the buyer's reward, as they are the ones who are blessed with ongoing appreciation of the finished artwork.
www.bellinifinemoulding.com.au

PHASEONE

Phase One is the main digital system I use and the Australian agents are L&P Digital Photographic www.lapfoto.com.au. If you want a truly professional system that sets you apart from the crowd go with Phase One and enjoy the ultimate image quality.
www.phaseone.com

ARB 4X4 ACCESSORIES

I travel extensively through some of Australia's most remote locations. For this I need the best equipment and there is nothing more trustworthy than ARB gear. From my IPF lights (to show the way) and drawers (that protect my gear) to my Warn winch that hauls me to safety, ARB keeps me out of trouble.
www.arb.com.au

EPSON EXCEED YOUR VISION

When it comes to inkjet printing technology Epson is without doubt the market leader. Whether for professional or home applications you can be guaranteed quality prints that will last. I believe there is no other inkjet process that can come close to the sharpness and colour reproduction of an Epson UltraChrome print.
www.epson.com.au

LUMIX™

Lumix Cameras from Panasonic really put the fun back into photography. I always carry one or more of these wonderful cameras for those spontaneous photo opportunities. The quality is so good that I can even use these images and amazing video footage for professional productions.
www.panasonic.com.au

The opinions Ken Duncan expresses in this book are his own and are not necessarily shared by these sponsors.

Torres Del Paine National Park, Chile

THOUGHT

Sometimes we have our own idea of how things should be.

I wanted a still lake with perfect reflections, but had to contend with a howling gale.

I doubted the shot above would work, but it did.

It reminds me that reality can often be larger than imagination – if we are open to change.

Brighton Beach huts, Vic

Sometimes I lie awake at night, and I ask,
"Where have I gone wrong?"
Then a voice says to me,
"This is going to take more than one night."
CHARLIE BROWN

Contents

7	Special Thanks	84	Divine Intervention
12	Introduction: Faith or Fear	86	It's Not about Us
14	Golden Days	46	You Can't Miss It	90	That's Ridiculous	126	Laughter is the Best Medicine
18	The Journey	50	Refuge Found	91	In God We Trust	128	Global Warming
22	Ned Kelly – Such is Life	52	Bureaucratic Bungle Bungles	92	The New Millennium	132	Patagonia Paradise
23	River Pirates	53	Sailing Away	97	I Still Call Australia Home	136	Photography Should be Fun
24	Country Living	58	Beware of the Gardener	98	Over the Edge	140	The Art of Photography
26	Protecting our History	60	Nebo's Dream for a Nation	102	Arts Freedom	142	Chasing Tigers
28	From Tragedy comes Hope	64	Overcoming Fear	104	Don't get Stuck in a Box	144	World Vision: Mother & Child
29	Get Big or Get Out	67	The Carnival	108	Wildlife Love Affair	151	Essential Oils
32	Simplicity of Life	69	The Circus comes to Town	116	Stuff Happens	154	Shining Light: New Zealand
33	Walkabout	72	Anger or Angels	118	Dipsticks of the Outback	157	China Awakens
36	Power and Passion	76	Go with the Flow	120	Our Island Paradise	160	Walk a While
43	High Country Heroes	78	A Gift	124	Letter to a Rich Man	162	Revival in the Heartland
		82	Getting out of Bed			166	Index of images
		83	The Dividing Line			168	Imprint

LIFE'S A JOURNEY 11

Introduction: Faith or Fear

One of my favourite sayings is "Life's an adventure, not a worry". In life, many difficulties arise and some threaten to overwhelm us, but I believe it's important to learn to dust ourselves off and keep going. Never give up; the adventure of life must continue.

Since 9/11, much of the world is constricted by fear and anxiety. If it's not some terrorist coming to get us, then it's the Global Financial Crisis; if not that, it's climate change, or some horrible new strain of flu. The list goes on, with new dangers added daily by the media. Everyday life has enough stress without all these added issues. I made a decision not to play the world's crippling fear game. So I felt it was time for a new book focusing on the adventure of life, to help knock this fear ball out of the park.

Another of my favourite sayings is "Faith or fear? It's your choice." I believe this is a key question for the age we live in. What will you choose? Fear that imprisons you, or faith that frees you?

The antidote to fear is faith, but faith in what? I choose faith based in the creator of the universe. The beauty of creation surrounds us all and my passion is to present the splendour of nature for others to enjoy. People often ask me to show them the creator. My answer is, "Really? Just open your eyes and look around."

Sometimes just when I think I've got a handle on how big the creator is, another grand and astounding aspect of creation will be revealed to me. I then hear my creator saying, "Ken, I am bigger than anything you can imagine and bigger than any problem or circumstance you may face."

The great thing about faith based in the creator, is that the world may take all you own – even your life – but it can never take your faith, unless you surrender it.

If our faith is based in worldly possessions, in finances, or in people, then we're in trouble. Things will come and things will go. Do we own our belongings or do they own us? If we lived our lives and used our gifts and possessions knowing one day we would stand before the creator and give an account of our lives, how would we change?

Some people want to blame the creator for lack or inequity. I think Mahatma Gandhi put it well when he said: "There is enough in the world for everyone's need, but not for everyone's greed."

Some people reject the concept of a creator because it raises the question of accountability. Whether or not we believe in a creator, we understand that human beings have free will. Logically, therefore, we must also understand that our choices have consequences. I believe there will be accountability for all our actions here on earth.

Doubt is the close relative of fear, and it, too, can quench the flame of faith. I know without doubt that the creator loves us and ultimately is in control. We live in a beautiful world, full of hope and promise. I see a great future for our planet. So, look up. The stars in the heavens above are a constant reminder that anything is possible.

Daily we have choices to make: Will we live our lives in faith or fear? I choose faith. Who will join me in this peaceful revolution?

Ken Duncan

Ken Duncan, OAM

PHOTO BY LUKE PETERSON

Golden Days

Many people tell me they wish they could do what I do – get paid to travel around the world taking photos in exciting locations. This is a fairly simplistic view of my job description. There are many aspects of my work that are difficult and some that are definitely not fun. But I won't dwell on those (since every job has them).

I am blessed that my passion is my occupation. In fact, someone once asked me what my hobby was. Without hesitation I said, "Photography." I was promptly told, "You can't have your hobby as your job." I answered, "Why not? Isn't one of the keys to fulfilment in life finding something you love doing and getting paid for it?"

Overall, I love the adventure of my life. Yet my wonderful wife and I have often had to put everything on the line to continue the journey. My wife, Pam, is my treasure beyond measure, and we share our adventures together. At times we both feel a bit overwhelmed, but our faith and our sense of excitement keep us going. Far better to have tried in life than to die wondering.

I believe the depth of our lives is determined more by the choices we make than by chance – although chance does often shine on the bold! Anyone can follow their dreams if they really want to. But first it is important to consider the cost.

You may have to invest all you have – and more – to bring your dreams to life. Often when you have a vision, doors don't open until you start walking in the direction you need to go. Many times I've wished I had all I needed to complete a dream before I started to walk it, but that easy road won't build great faith. The pieces of the puzzle will be provided only as we dare to use whatever we have to pursue our dream.

The journey my wife and I have taken is not for everyone; it's the journey we've chosen. It's no greater than anyone else's story – in fact, I'm often in awe of the many adventurers I meet along the way. Sometimes those who live the simplest lives of all have the most to say. I believe everyone has a purpose in life and a reason for being on this beautiful planet. Before leaving earth, it's great to find out what your mission is and to give it a go with all you've got.

Our physical bodies seek comfort and control. There's nothing wrong with seeking worldly possessions or stability, but these can limit the journey of our spirit. It takes faith and courage to follow our dreams since our purpose often lies beyond the prison of our fears and understanding. As the great female aviator Amelia Earhart said: "Courage is the price that life exacts for granting peace." For me, peace comes when I know I'm doing what I'm called to do.

As a child, one of the main things that inspired me to follow my dream was looking at the old black and white photos my dad had taken. These pictures (shown on the following pages) captivated me. They were from the "golden days" when my parents had truly been pursuing their own vision. Mum and Dad worked with indigenous people in the remote Kimberley region back in the late 1940s. They were there to help train the people with skills that would give them greater opportunities for the future. Many of the present day cowboys of the Kimberley are descendants of men my father trained. When I visited the Kimberley – many years later – and met some of my parents'

James Duncan on horseback, Kunmunya, WA

Tribesmen, Kunmunya, WA

Watt Leggatt pearling lugger, Kimberley coast, WA

old friends from the past, I discovered my mum and dad were greatly loved there. It shouldn't have surprised me. My dad was a very humble man who never boasted of anything he had done in his past. He was also one of the most peaceful men I have ever known. And my mother is a lover of people, always seeing the best in everyone.

In my father's latter years he developed dementia. He couldn't remember much, but he could always recognise the picture of himself on his horse in the Kimberley. Why did he remember that picture? It was because that image represented a golden time in his life, when he and his young bride put everything on the line. In 2012 my dad passed away, but his legacy lives on.

When we dare to follow our dreams, the repercussions go beyond the lives of the dreamers – they leave seed for future generations. I am extremely thankful to my mum and dad for daring to pursue their dreams, and for helping to give our family the faith and courage to pursue ours.

Reconciliation in action, Kunmunya, WA

THOUGHT

*Heroes are often just regular people who don't allow any-
thing to stop them from helping others.
I thank God for my parents, who instilled in me the courage
to follow their lead in loving other people.
We find true meaning in life when we use what we have
to help those around us.*

Neta Duncan, WA

The Journey

The Old Fella has passed away now. I call him "The Old Fella" out of respect, for it is a custom of the Aboriginal people not to mention a person by name after their death.

I first met The Old Fella in Derby, which was the launching point for an expedition that I was undertaking with my father and our dear friend Howard into a remote region of the Kimberley. The Old Fella was a full-blood Aboriginal, an elder of his tribe. The area we were setting out to explore had been his home some twenty-five years earlier. My father and Howard had first known him in the time before indigenous people were taken from their tribal lands and placed in settlements.

With our four-wheel drive loaded with fuel, supplies and camera equipment, we made our first stop at Mount Elizabeth Station. From there we had to force a track to the abandoned Pantijana Station, more than 200 kilometres to the north. Here the formidable terrain blocked our path, so we made the decision to leave the vehicle and continue on foot. We carried some basic rations, but, in order to keep our packs as light as possible, we intended to live mainly off the land. My dad and Howard began studying their survey map to decide how best to access an area that Howard had last visited twenty-five years earlier. The Old Fella was bewildered at the white man's attempt to plot a course by looking at lines and squiggles on a piece of paper. However, when they had finally decided on a course, The Old Fella nodded in agreement – just to get the journey underway, I think.

As there are relatively few outstanding landmarks in this region on which to get a bearing, we kept as straight a course as possible. It was a hard slog through wild country, and so intent were we on reaching our destination that the journey itself became an affliction. To make matters worse, The Old Fella kept falling behind, as if he were being dragged away from an old friend.

On the fourth day, we were standing on the crest of a hill trying to get our bearings for the next stage, when The Old Fella finally spoke up. "You show me what you're aiming for," he said. "I'll meet you there and find some bush tucker on the way." So he went his own way. Sure enough, when we got to our next destination, The Old Fella was already there, holding some lily roots he had gathered. In contrast to us stubborn white fellas, who dumped our packs in sheer exhaustion, he looked relaxed and refreshed. From that point on, we decided to follow The Old Fella's lead. Although we kept to our schedule, the whole journey changed in character – from an effort into an adventure. It was like walking through nature's supermarket as we watched The Old Fella gather all kinds of different foods along the way. My favourite was bush honey.

After a week of travelling, however, I began to feel restless and impatient to reach our final destination. I asked The Old Fella how far we still had to go. He answered, "Little bit long way, maybe one jump-up, maybe two." (A jump-up was his term for a hill.) By midday the next day we still had not arrived and I asked again, "How much further?" He gave me the same reply, "Little bit long way, maybe one jump-up, maybe two." Barely curbing my anger and frustration, I walked on. The next day I asked for the last time. "Okay, Old Fella. How much further?" His predictable reply was delivered right on cue. "That's it," I exploded. "I want to know exactly how far we still have to go!" He looked at me with soft eyes and said, "Does it

Daisy, Violet, Ken and Djomery, Derby, WA

matter? Isn't the journey as important as the destination?" Talk about a man of few words! What could I say? He was right, of course. I had been so obsessed with reaching a particular place that I was failing to appreciate the journey.

We finally arrived, and we made some even greater discoveries along the way. But these were secondary to the lesson I had learned from The Old Fella: the journey should always be as important as the destination. If you don't enjoy the journey, is there any point in getting to your destination? It is, after all, the journey that gives the destination its real meaning.

Mitchell Falls, WA

LIFE'S A JOURNEY   21

Kelly homestead ruins, Glenrowan, Vic

Ned Kelly – Such is Life

It was Christmas Day, and my wife and I were photographing for my first book. We camped by the roadside near the ruins of Ned Kelly's parents' homestead in Glenrowan. Christmas at Ned's place – how much more Australian could you get?

We both remember this place well. The weather was very hot and dry and while cooking our breakfast we accidentally set fire to the grass! We had to move quickly to bring the fire under control and avoid a major bushfire.

When we recovered from that excitement, I wandered over to the old Kelly ruins and tried to imagine some of the good times Ned might have had here before his notoriety.

Ned Kelly was the son of an Irish convict father, and, as a young man, he clashed with Victorian police. Following an incident at this home (pictured) in 1878, police squads searched for Ned in the bush. Ned killed three policemen, and he and his gang were proclaimed outlaws by the colony.

We may never completely know what caused Ned Kelly to become an outlaw. Some hail him as a folk hero – a symbol of Irish-Australian resistance against an Anglo-Australian ruling class. Others consider him a cold-blooded killer. Personally I wonder what made him snap.

A final violent confrontation with police took place at Glenrowan on 28 June 1880. Kelly, dressed in homemade metal armour, was captured and jailed. Convicted on three counts of wilful murder, he was hanged in November at Old Melbourne Gaol. His parting words: "Such is Life".

Paddle steamer on the Murray River, Vic

River Pirates

I was born on the Murray, near where my farming ancestors loaded paddle steamers with wool for market. To this day, I feel a strong connection to that river.

With my fertile imagination, I was sure there were river pirates and therefore treasures to be found. In fact, I believed our *neighbour* was a pirate. His wife had gone missing and I was sure he'd "done her in" and was waiting for the cover of darkness to remove her body and bury his treasure. (I admit my favourite book at the time was *Treasure Island*.)

I was convinced this pirate was up to no good so, at the mature age of seven, I would sneak out at night to case his lair.

One night, under a full moon, I caught the pirate out. He and an accomplice were man-handling a canvas-covered, body-sized package into his boat, along with a large box that I was sure was a treasure chest.

I raced home and woke my dad. (I knew my limitations when it came to two big pirates.) My gracious dad went out to investigate the matter. When he returned he could barely suppress his laughter as he told me, "Ken that was Old Thommo and his mate. They're fishermen! In the bag were nets; the big box has their fishing gear. And his missing wife is away looking after her sick father."

Well, they may have fooled my dad, but I'm still sure they were river pirates.

Sheep muster, Korumburra, Vic

Country Living

A rural environment is a great place to raise a family. I was blessed to be raised in the country and I have many wonderful memories of that time. We were lucky enough to live on an agricultural research station and therefore had lots of animals and plenty of space for adventures.

When I was around seven years old, my two older sisters, Jennifer and Anne, taught me to drive. The vehicle was an old car – pretty much a wreck – that had a milk crate in place of the driver's seat. My biggest problem was seeing over the steering wheel. The car had no brakes, but the paddock that became my driving course was flat, so we would stop the car by running into the corner of a haystack. It was all fairly painless.

My sisters also taught me how to ride a bike. They took me up a track onto a hill that was the highest point on the farm. My well-meaning instructors helped me climb up onto the seat of a large girls' bike and the lesson went like this: "See these handlebars, they steer the bike. Now just keep your feet on the pedals and away you go."

So off I went, wobbling a lot at first, but soon I was flying down the hill. There was just one problem; the girls had forgotten to tell me how to slow down or stop and there was no haystack in site.

In the yards, Korumburra, Vic

So I aimed for the barn. I've heard it said that some people can't hit the broad side of a barn – but I hit it just fine and rocketed in through the open doors, bouncing from object to object. Eventually, I came to a stop – a little battered, but alive. My dad was close by and caught sight of me disappearing into the barn at high speed with a very worried look on my face. When he heard the impact he came running, along with my sisters. As Dad untangled me from the mess, my sisters stood sheepishly by the doors taking in the carnage. When Dad asked what in the world we thought we were doing, my sisters replied: "We forgot to tell him about the brakes."

Farmer's daughter, Wentworth, NSW

Protecting our History

Burra is a pretty little town, nestled in a valley 160 kilometres north of Adelaide and surrounded by rolling hills. When copper was discovered in the banks of Burra Burra Creek way back in 1845, the township grew quickly as thousands of immigrants flocked to the region to work the rich copper lode. By 1850, Burra was Australia's largest inland settlement, with the Burra copper mine making a significant contribution to South Australia's early prosperity.

When copper production slowed in the 1870s, Burra's prosperity continued as it evolved into an important regional agricultural service hub and a centre for sheep-breeding. Today, tourism is also an important industry. Visitors come to wander amongst the magnificent collection of historic buildings that give a rare insight into the life and times of Australia's early settlement.

I first discovered this fascinating town in the 1980s. But who would have imagined, when I photographed the classic old homestead at Burra all those years ago, that it would become one of South Australia's major tourist icons. One of my photos of the cottage was used for the cover of Midnight Oil's album *Diesel and Dust*, and since then the homestead has appeared in many promotions, including the Qantas campaign *I still call Australia home*, which was shown on TV all around the world.

Now the old homestead at Burra is in trouble. Storms have begun to lift the roof off the building and urgent restoration work is needed to avert further damage. There is a great deal of history attached to this humble dwelling and it would be a shame to see it crumble into the ground. But that's what will happen if the roof comes off. I have seen it many times before. When the roof is gone, the walls quickly start falling.

That is exactly what happened to Old Halls Creek Post Office in Western Australia (page 28). When the roof came off that building, nothing was done about it. Without a roof for protection, it didn't take long before much of the mud brick structure began to crumble. Bureaucracy sometimes moves at the speed of a slug and often more money is spent forming a committee than it would take to fix the problem. In the end, a large roof was put up over the whole post office site (which would have cost a fortune). Sadly, it is a really ugly structure. It is a pity the bureaucrats didn't move more quickly – the building could have been preserved in a far better state for future generations to appreciate.

Fortunately, a group of concerned locals have joined together to raise funds for the "Burra Homestead (Midnight Oil Cottage) Restoration Project". They did seek financial assistance from the government, but were denied because the homestead is on private land. I feel for the farmer who owns this land. Tourists come from far and wide to see the cottage, often trampling any crop he has planted close to the place. The farmer is not looking to repair the homestead so he can live in it, but to preserve it for posterity. I'm passionate about protecting our history, so I've pledged to do all I can to raise awareness – and funds – to assist with the restoration project. If you would like to help, you can contact midnightoilcottage@gmail.com

With support from the wider community, the committed citizens group will no doubt get the job done and dusted, proving yet again that the great Aussie spirit can conquer just about anything.

Reggies Hut, Burra, SA

Burra Homestead, SA

Old Halls Creek Post Office, WA

From Tragedy comes Hope

One day in 1917, Jimmy Darcy, a stockman at Ruby Plains Station, fell from his horse and was seriously injured. His friends took him by buggy to Halls Creek (a twelve-hour journey) but there was no doctor or hospital in the town. The local postmaster, F.W. Tuckett, had sufficient medical knowledge to realise that Darcy needed immediate medical attention. He telegraphed Dr Holland in Perth who diagnosed Darcy as having a ruptured bladder.

Messages flashed back and forth in Morse code. "You must operate." "But I have no instruments." "You have a penknife and razor." "What about drugs?" "Use permanganate of potash." "I can't do it." "You must." "But I might kill the man." "If you don't hurry, the patient will die."

Tuckett strapped Darcy to the table. Then – without anaesthetic – he operated for seven hours according to the instructions he received by telegraph. A day later, complications set in. The doctor from Perth would have to come to Halls Creek. Dr Holland took about two weeks to arrive, only to find that Darcy had died the day before.

Dr Holland performed an autopsy and reported that Darcy hadn't died as a result of his injury, nor from the effects of Tuckett's surgery. Tragically, Darcy had not fully recovered from a previous bout of malaria, and as he lay in Halls Creek the fever had returned with fatal virility.

Darcy's plight had not only focused the entire nation on the problems of medical services in isolated areas, but it also inspired Rev. John Flynn to establish the Royal Flying Doctor Service.

Farmer harvesting, NSW

Get Big or Get Out

A prestigious New York magazine invited me to shoot for a feature article on wheat farming in Western Australia. The text they sent was written in a new-age esoteric style. Even the wheat had emotions. So I headed to the wild west to shoot "Zen and the art of wheat farming".

It was the 1980s and many of Western Australia's wheat farmers had gone big – large farms with millions invested in huge harvesters and other machinery. Many were working hard just to pay their banks. This was not the greatest place to find Zen farming techniques, or wheat with personality, but, being a pro, I got some images that would satisfy the brief.

Assignment over, back in New South Wales, I ran into this character working his wheat fields with a classic old Massey Ferguson harvester. I asked what his story was. He said: "Some politician named Doug Anthony came and gave us farmers a talk; he said, 'Get big or get out.' Well a lot of people followed his advice – they borrowed big and went out the back door. I decided to keep things simple. I have my own seed, not that genetic stuff others have to buy each year; I own my farm and all my equipment. It's more labour intensive and has lower yields, but I have a couple of sons. I have to give them something to keep them out of trouble."

I loved this great Aussie farmer. If I were wheat with feelings, I would hang out on his farm.

Sugarcane fire, Qld

What you fear, becomes your master.

KEN DUNCAN

Kimberley kids, Cape Leveque, WA.

Simplicity of Life

I love my many indigenous friends – they often have a unique concept of time. They never allow themselves to be imprisoned by it.

I was shooting for the big Qantas advertising campaign *I still call Australia home*. We were at Cape Leveque, with lots of young singers and a large film crew. The casting agent had organised for a couple of indigenous kids from a nearby community to join the cast. I asked when they would be coming and she said, very confidently, "Eight o'clock tomorrow morning." Wow – so positive. I was impressed.

At 9am the next morning everyone was waiting to start filming but no indigenous kids had arrived. So I asked the agent if she would like me to go and see what had happened to them. I grabbed a small bus and drove down to the community, where I learned that our young stars had gone fishing. Clearly they considered that a better offer. Fortunately, one of the tribal elders of that community was a good friend of mine and when I explained the problem, she came with me and helped me fill the bus with kids of all ages and sizes.

When we arrived on set, the crew was amazed how many kids we had, and the day's shooting went well. By sunset, we were all exhausted from having so much fun, and we looked on, mesmerised, as the sun slipped into the sea. We had all had the time of our lives.

Sliding rock, Yirrkala, NT

Walkabout

In the modern world, many of our youth seem to need numerous playthings to keep themselves amused. These children at Yirrkala made their own fun by simply sliding down a smooth rock into the tepid sea. To get this shot, I first had to gain the trust of the kids by sliding with them. It took time to get real connection. When my shorts were almost worn through, they allowed me to photograph them at play.

From these children we can learn some important lessons, both on relationships and on the simplicity of life. These days, sadly, it's not only our youth who need multiple toys. Without our techno gadgets, we can all feel we've been disconnected from life, when in fact the opposite is true.

From time to time I like to go on "Walkabout Incommunicado" – intentionally cutting myself off from electronic communications. Anyone who knows me well, knows this about me: If I don't respond quickly to a call or email, I'm either out of range or in techno hibernation.

I believe that when we're overloaded with input, we need time out to process for the "gold". My indigenous friends call this time *Walkabout* – what we might call simply "time out". It helps clear our minds so we can really connect with nature or enter that truly creative zone.

Thank you to all my friends – young and old – for all you've shown me about taking time to connect with both land and people.

Mel Gibson, Tangambalanga, Vic

LIFE'S A JOURNEY   35

Power and Passion

Mel Gibson and I have been good friends since we were about eighteen. He has always been a larrikin and a dreamer and I found it hard to relate to him as the great driver in *Mad Max*. I remember the young Mel, who would be dreaming so much – even while driving – that he would sometimes miss a stop sign. He would just sail on through, with the traffic around him doing seemingly magical diversions. His passengers' blood-curdling screams would thankfully bring him back to earth, and he would ask: "What's up?" He was a lucky young man, no doubt, and I thought it a miracle that he survived.

When we left school, Mel was the "starving artist" following his passion, and I became the businessman seeking money and possessions. Mel visited me at work one day and told me he felt he should settle down – maybe take a television role for a more regular income. I said, "Don't do it; don't let go of your big movie dream. What I have may look good but, really, it sucks."

It wasn't long after this that Mel got his movie break. He headed to Los Angeles to follow his star and soon after that I sold up and went walkabout in the Australian outback. I thought it would only take me three months to photograph Australia, but I disappeared for three years as I learned to capture the beauty of creation in panoramic format. When I returned to Sydney I contacted Mel, who had meanwhile become a superstar. He was still the same mate I had known with a heart of gold, which has always been his greatest asset.

I am very proud of how Mel has stood up over the years to the trials and tribulations he has been through. The movies he has made are tribute to his tenacity and to his talent as an actor and director and I know that many more great works will come from this man. Mel has been a tremendous blessing to me over the years. Watching his life has helped me learn a lot of lessons without me having to go through the same ordeals.

Many people desire riches and fame, but I have seen how difficult that road can be. It is a tough world and there are a thousand spotlights aimed at anyone who takes the stage. The Pandora's box of possibilities presented to people in positions of power or influence can be overwhelming.

Over the years Mel and I have shared some special times. This shoot was one such time. Mel wanted out of the movie industry for a while so he decided to become "Farmer Brown" and get back to earth. He bought an awesome cattle farm in Victoria.

In 1987 Mel met a local guy, Rob Taylor, who was running as an independent candidate for their area in the federal election. Mel liked Rob's family values so he got behind his campaign. When the media became aware of Mel's endorsement, Rob started getting huge publicity – talk about a "Lethal Weapon".

I headed down to Mel's farm to see what was happening. At the farm Mel received a threatening phone call from one of the heads of the Labor party at that time. Mel was told he needed to "stay with acting and get out of politics" or action would be taken against him. One comment went something like this, "We'll find problems with your taxes." Obviously the Labor party was concerned about the impact Mel's involvement was having on their candidate's chances.

Farmer Mel

LIFE'S A JOURNEY 37

Mel Gibson on the farm, Tangambalanga, Vic

Mel got off the phone, clearly shaken and upset, and told me what had transpired. "Can you believe a government leader would threaten me, just because I stand up for someone?" he asked. "What sort of country has this become?" That incident left a barb in Mel's heart, and, I believe, was one of the reasons he left Australia to live in America.

To Mel's credit he didn't back down because of the threats. He went to a rally to support Rob Taylor and here are some of the images of that "Brave Heart" time.

The issue here is not about Liberal or Labor. It's about integrity – or the lack of it – in politics. Are we a nation that condones the threatening of people who have an opinion? A politician friend of mine recently said, "Politics is the hardest game to play. You often have to compromise something you believe in to get something else for the greater good." I replied, "You need to be careful. If you start compromising your core beliefs and the policies you were voted in for, then there is no greater good."

There are many politicians with high integrity – and many more who started out that way. But too often they allow party politics to compromise their beliefs. We need integrity and accountability from those in power. With great power comes even greater responsibility – and if people don't use their power to benefit others, it will consume them.

Mel at political rally, Wodonga, Vic

Mel supporting independent candidate Robert Taylor

*Sometimes I wonder whether the world is being run
by smart people who are putting us on,
or by imbeciles who really mean it.*

MARK TWAIN

Snow gums, Alpine National Park, Vic

THOUGHT

*I believe great photos are gifts given to those who are willing to spend time relating to their surroundings.
I nearly drove right past the scene above; my natural mind saw only trees and mist,
but something in my spirit was alerted. Listening to such feelings can bring great blessing.*

Brumbies at dawn, Benambra, Vic

Stockman's hut, Falls Creek, Vic

High Country Heroes

High country cattlemen are part of our heritage – an integral part of the "DNA" that makes us a strong and resilient nation. If Australia ever found itself in difficult times, these are the types of tough, resourceful people I would want around.

One of our famous poets, A.B. "Banjo" Paterson, was so impressed by these high country heroes, that he immortalised their character in his legendary poem "The Man from Snowy River".

Much has changed since that poem was written. Most of our high country regions have been declared state or national parks. These days, the very heroes who made the high country famous, and cared for it for so long, are fighting park authorities and politicians for access. I feel sorry for the new generation of cowboys and cowgirls. They are being taught the skills but are locked out of the areas their ancestors worked in.

Visitors delight in our classic high country cattlemen's cottages. People want to connect with that heritage. To perpetuate the cattlemen's legends, some of our parks spend considerable money and effort maintaining these historic huts. They keep the huts and the history, but kick out the builders and their descendants. To me, this is a case of bureaucracy gone mad.

For generations, high country cattle workers grazed their cattle or mustered wild brumbies in the highlands in the warmer seasons. This practice kept the undergrowth to controllable levels, which helped reduce the intensity of fires that can decimate the forests.

Our early indigenous people managed forests by regularly lighting fires to prevent the undergrowth getting to dangerous levels. Fortunately they are still able to manage large areas of Australia with their traditions, yet our high country pioneers are locked out.

Management policies seem to turn huge areas into parks, then limit access as much as possible. Because the areas are so vast, and their resources and budgets limited, the authorities cannot successfully manage the parks. They find themselves overwhelmed with the problems of feral animals, non-native vegetation and general policing of all the rules. In recent years, due partly to park authorities' failure to fully manage the areas, we have lost thousands of hectares of forest that may not regenerate. We also lost some huts because of the intensity of bushfires. It will take years for nature to heal the scars.

What happened to the Aussie spirit of co-operation? It used to be that people with historical connections worked with those responsible for protecting these areas. Park staff used to be our allies in the protection of our environment, but now, with their higher education, some have their heads in the clouds of their own self-importance. Many of our park rangers are great people but are also overwhelmed by the bureaucracy that has overtaken the system. It's no longer about the staff's connection to the land; it's about how many degrees they have in hand. Many are so busy being politically correct and buried in paperwork on the ladder to success, they have little time to actually manage the parks.

What makes Australia such a strong nation is that we will only take so much. Then we stand up and say, "Enough."

I am hearing the echoes of wild brumbies galloping through the bush, with the crack of a stockman's whip reverberating in the air. We still have the spirit of the high country heroes in our blood. So let's keep the whips a-cracking, that common sense may again rein in the wild horses.

Aerial, Lawn Hill, Qld

LIFE'S A JOURNEY 45

You Can't Miss It

Travelling through the Queensland Gulf Country, shooting for my first book, *The Last Frontier*, Pam and I met some fantastic people and had many great adventures.

After the heat and dust of the arid gulf area, the desert paradise of Lawn Hill Gorge was a wonderful find. It had camping facilities, good canoeing and swimming – it was just a great place to hang out.

While we were canoeing on the river one day, a helicopter buzzed very low overhead. We discovered it had come from Lawn Hill Station, where they were mustering cattle.

We drove to the station and met with the manager. His speech was so slow that I thought he was making fun of us because we were "city slickers". But he was a really nice guy, and when he heard our story he said I could go up with one of the mustering pilots for free, if I was game. He said, "All our pilots have *had the operation*." "What's that?" I asked, and he replied, "They've had their brains and nerves removed." I was soon to find out exactly what he meant.

The next morning at the mustering briefing, I met the pilot I would be flying with. His nickname was "Biggles". Despite the station manager's slow speech (which I found out was his normal way of speaking), Biggles and I finally got into the air. He threw his helicopter all over the place as he chased the cattle – and he kept looking at me to see how I was faring. As he powered into a vertical climb, the helicopter stalled, and then, as it began to drop, the engine started again. I had never had such an exhilarating flight. Biggles looked over and asked, "Are you all right?" I replied, "Sure, why?" Biggles told me, "I've been trying to put the wind up you, but you seem to be enjoying it! Aren't you afraid we might crash?" Surprised, I answered, "Well, I thought you must know what you're doing because if we crash, we'll probably both be killed." From that time on, Biggles and I got on fine. He was a talented pilot.

After our adventures at Lawn Hill Station, Pam and I set off towards Burketown via a place Biggles had told us was special. His instructions went like this: "After you cross the second creek, look for a fence and follow it down about ten kilometres. You can't miss it." Pam was sick and needed to get to a doctor, but we wanted to find this special location on our way to Burketown.

Many creeks later, we had obviously missed it and were headed into the Never Never. Much later, we found out the fence was just a wire on the ground since the fence posts burned down in a bush fire. So we were lost, with only half a tank of fuel. Should we go back, or go on looking for a way to Burketown? There were no signs and no GPS. All I had were some old survey maps. I got out my compass and decided to head on.

The track I had found began to widen, which lifted my spirits. But then, flying around a corner, I was faced with a deep wash-out, half a metre wide, right across the road. With no chance of stopping in time, I floored the accelerator and tried to jump the obstacle. We landed with a big thump. Pam got airborne in the back, as various objects sailed through the air around her, but fortunately landed on the bed. I thought we had pulled it off. Then I looked down at my oil gauge and watched the needle sink to the left. We'd lost oil pressure. I got out to investigate and discovered a hole in my engine sump. I fixed the split in the sump with some soap and filled up with spare oil so we could keep going. We made it to a remote aboriginal

Lawn Hill Creek, Qld

Lawn Hill Gorge, Lawn Hill National Park, Qld

Albert Hotel, Burketown, Qld

community where we bought more fuel and oil and got directions to Burketown, still 160 kilometres away.

Back on the road again, after only a few kilometres, my car kept jumping out of gear. So I got out to investigate. It wasn't good. The engine of my Toyota Land Cruiser was balanced on the front diff. Our hard landing after the jump across the wash-out had snapped some of the engine mounts. Pam, who by that time was really sick, called out from the back to ask what was happening. "Nothing too bad, dear," I replied, "but the engine is falling out and I'll have to rope it in." With no passing traffic to ask for help on this outback track, I set to work. Once the engine was roped in, we set off again, but at a top speed of thirty kilometres per hour.

A short while later, I saw a car broken down on the track. An aboriginal was using a small tree trunk to try to lever the engine out of his car – with no success. He was dangling in the air. When I stopped and asked if I could help, he told me he and his mates were trying to fix his engine which had "a bit of a knocking noise". One look told me why it had a knocking noise. The piston shaft had knocked its way through the side of the engine block. So I towed this guy and his mates to Burketown.

We finally made it. Our new indigenous friends were grateful for the helping hand but we were exhausted after a long, tiring day. Pam was really sick by this time, so I took her to the hospital. The nurse there asked where we were staying and when I said we were going to find a place to camp, she said, "No way! This girl needs a bed. You'll be staying at the pub for at least a couple of nights."

The pub owners, Tex and Lorraine, are two of the loveliest people we have ever met – true "salt of the earth" folk. Lorraine cared for Pam as if she was her own daughter – in fact, Pam started calling her Mum after a few days.

The Burketown locals also helped me fix my car. They were such friendly people and they pretty much adopted us; we stayed with them for many days while we checked out the surrounding area.

So what lessons did we learn from that trip? Firstly, be careful of pilots who have *had the operation*. And secondly, when people in the outback say, "You can't miss it", get them to draw you an accurate map to the place. The photo on this page is a tribute to the many beautiful, yet-to-be-discovered places that we *did* miss with dodgy directions.

Refuge Cove, Vic

Refuge Found

Wilsons Promontory in Victoria is a place I'd always wanted to visit by boat to explore all the beautiful locations I knew were there. In 1991, I met up with a really interesting guy who had the perfect yacht – a catamaran. It was fast and stable and provided a great base to work from. The skipper knew the Promontory well and was excited when I chartered his vessel for our quest.

We arrived at this stunning bay called Refuge Cove – a favourite haven for sailors who needed to take refuge from the dangerous southern seas, or for those who simply wanted to chill out.

It was an idyllic place. We could just back up to the shoreline and step onto the glorious beach. To top it off, the boat owner was an amazing cook. He got the barbeque cranking on the aft deck and delivered all kinds of mouth-watering delights. Deliciously cold bottles of beer were handed around to wash it all down. How refreshing. This was not just a haven – more like heaven on earth.

After many days away, we were nearing the end of our trip. We were in quite a euphoric state; there in the wonderful Aussie sunshine, we were having such a relaxing time we just wanted the adventure to continue. In fact, we were having so many laughs we started to feel a bit guilty (not one of us with a Catholic upbringing!) and began to wonder what the rest of the world was up to. Mind you, we didn't intend to invite them to our party.

Refuge beach, Vic

Suddenly, I had a great idea. "Let's find a news station," I said, looking at the catamaran's radio, "and see what's happening in the big wide world."

We found a station with a strong signal and the news erupted loud and clear.

"The United States and coalition forces have launched a massive military assault on Iraq, and on Iraqi forces in Kuwait." The newsreader went on to describe in detail the brutality and hardships people were facing. Then he rolled out interviews with specialists and analysts. They were expressing their fears that this incident could trigger other nations to join in the battle. They went on and on, giving a blow-by-blow account of what was unfolding. In the end we had to turn the radio off. What could we do from so far away, other than pray for all involved?

Talk about sobering. We just sat back looking at each other, and said, "How lucky are we?" We were in paradise, and on the other side of the planet a war was raging.

We are tremendously blessed to live in such a beautiful nation as Australia and to have the opportunities we have. All of us who call Australia home – no matter where we have come from or what our beliefs are – must learn to live in peace. Unity will bring growth, but division can only cause destruction. May war never touch our shores.

Bungle Bungles, Purnululu National Park, WA

Bureaucratic Bungle Bungles

In 1982, people began talking about a new place found in the Kimberley called the Bungle Bungles. I decided to check it out. There were no real roads into the area as yet, so I hired a helicopter to go exploring. I got some shots and determined to return at a later date. Back then there were no people anywhere near the place. Locals actually referred to the area as "badlands" because if their cattle got into the labyrinth of domes and gorges, they were very difficult to find.

By the time I returned about six years later, everyone wanted a piece of those badlands because the area had been declared a national park and there was money to be made. Rangers were trying to sort through ownership claims from different indigenous groups and trying to decide on a name for the new park. In those days the rangers were still pretty friendly. Although their arrival brought reams of rules and regulations, they were willing to work with photographers to help us get some good shots to promote the park.

Since then, I've visited numerous times. What concerns me is that each time I go, there are more and more restrictions on what you can do and where you can go. Bureaucracy is threatening to choke the life out of the place.

Just like our indigenous Australians, we all need connection to the land. For the land unites us all, and that link can bring comfort to all our souls.

Great Barrier Reef, Qld

Sailing Away

A cartoon by Aussie artist Michael Leunig impacted me in my younger days. It showed a father and son, sitting together in a room, watching a sunset on television. Off to the side, through the window of the room, you could see the same sunset they were watching on TV. It was happening for real just outside, but father and son were mesmerised by that television.

How many times do we get caught up in living our lives vicariously, rather than experiencing things in reality? Do we allow our children to live their lives through multimedia devices? Life should be an adventure that we are immersed in – not just a virtual reality.

That's why I love photography – it forces me get outside into creation. And I love bringing the splendour of creation back for others, in the hope it will inspire them to follow their dreams.

Here, someone is daring to live their dream. Many people dream of sailing away and scenes like this make the dream even more appealing. Anchored within Hardy Reef, the yacht's occupants look out upon crystal clear waters teeming with tropical life. It's a veritable paradise. But how many storms has this craft had to weather and how much preparation has gone before this day of glory?

Life is full of character-building situations. As we face them, we get to experience such exotic moments as this. These people haven't found themselves here simply by chance, but through the choices they have made.

Hill Inlet, Whitsunday Island, Qld

Courage is the price that life exacts for granting peace.
AMELIA EARHART

Cameron Highlands, Malaysia

There is more to life than increasing its speed.

MAHATMA GANDHI

Beware of the Gardener

Forty-six photographers selected from the world's top magazines and photo agencies, were invited to shoot for a major book project in Malaysia. I was rather surprised to be one of the photographers chosen. Surrounded by such famous people, I felt totally out of my league.

It was 1989. Before commencing our various assignments around the country, we had to attend numerous formal functions, which included thanking the sponsors and even meeting Malaysia's President of the time, Dr Mahathir Mohamad.

When we arrived at the President's palace to meet him, the project leader asked if I would take a group shot of all the photographers with the President. I was concerned about having to shoot all those great photographers, but tried not to let that show. While everyone else went off to meet the President, I stayed out in the gardens to find a location for the panoramic group shot. As fortune would have it, the best place to take the shot from was right in the middle of a spiky fern garden.

While I was setting up for the shot, standing precariously atop my camera case for height, along came a guy who looked to me like the gardener and asked what I was doing there. I explained that a whole group of photographers had come to meet the President but I didn't really care about that sort of thing, as I had to do a group shot. "Unfortunately this is the spot that gives me the best angle," I said. He was intrigued and wanted to see what my camera was seeing. Trying to avoid the spikes, I helped him up on my case to look through the viewfinder and he said, "Wow, now I see." He was a friendly fellow, so I asked him what it was like being a gardener. He laughed and said, "Oh no, I'm not the gardener. I'm the President of Malaysia." I replied, "Right. No wonder your English is so good! So what's it like to be the President?" He was very gracious and we had a few good laughs. The others who had gone to see the President had obviously not found him. As they were being led out to where we were, one of my friends grabbed a quick shot of me with Mr President.

I took this shot with me on my assignment up into the Cameron Highlands, thinking it might help if I had any problems. We also carried letters of introduction from Malaysia's high-ranking officials, requesting that people give us all possible assistance.

Part of my assignment was to negotiate a treacherous jungle track up near the Thailand border, to photograph the people of the Orang Asli tribe. These people were still very primitive, hunting with blowpipes and poisoned darts. On arrival at the checkpoint into the area, I showed my paperwork to the offical, who said, simply, "You're not going." I explained that the project had the endorsement of the President of Malaysia and showed him the photo of me with Mr President. I felt sure he couldn't refuse. His response to that was, "Politicians come and politicians go, but we bureaucrats always remain."

Fortunately, the King of that area heard of my plight and came to my rescue. He personally drove me along the jungle track in his luxurious 4WD vehicle, as he knew all the people in the area. It was great when we arrived at the checkpoint and the same pompous offical was still there. He looked at the King and at my smiling face and begrudgingly said, "Go on through." It's good to know the King.

Fisherman, Penang, Malaysia

THOUGHT

It is wise to treat everyone with respect, because you never know who you may be talking to. And be careful what you say about others, as what is said will echo long after the words are spoken. The words we speak have power to bring life or to ignite a forest.

Ken with former Malaysian Prime Minister Dr Mahathir Mohamad

LIFE'S A JOURNEY   59

Nebo's Dream for a Nation

I was in Los Angeles, attending the wedding of my friend's daughter. Miracle or menace of our modern world, my mobile phone rang. It was Alison, one of my friends from Haasts Bluff (a remote aboriginal community in the Northern Territory). She had called to tell me The Old Fella had passed away. Out of respect so soon after his passing, the man's name could not be mentioned, but I knew who she was talking about. Sorrow hit me immediately. I was on the other side of the earth, but I could feel her pain and the pain of many others who would be affected by the passing of this beautiful elder of their tribe. I wanted to be with the community but was too far away. Despite the physical separation, I felt keenly connected to my Haasts Bluff friends and this tragic event.

My mind was racing. Should I drop everything and leave now? I had a commitment to be at the wedding. What could I do? Then suddenly, in the midst of that storm of emotions, a wonderful peace came over me. I was taken back to the time I went with that old man to the top of a mountain in his tribal country. It was his special place and he had taken me there as a treat. I fondly remembered the hours we had spent there, with Haasts Bluff looming in the background. We talked of many things that were happening in the community and he shared with me his concerns for the future. I now believe he knew that he would soon pass away, so he was sharing his knowledge. I knew at the time there was unfinished business between us, but I thought I would see him again. Now that he was gone, how could our unfinished business take place?

Late that night, my mind was whirling as I drifted off to sleep. In that place between sleeping and waking, I began to feel the presence of my old friend and hear his voice. I could see him on a mountaintop and he was speaking to me from that special place he had shown me, but we were separated by a big valley. I could hear him sharing with me stories of the hopes and fears he had for his people. I did not hear him with my natural ears but the stories came through the ground, through which we were both connected. Enough time has passed since his death that I can now tell you my friend's name was Nebo. This is what he said to me.

"Don't worry about our unfinished business. I have placed the stories in the land at the place I took you to. Listen now. Tell my people it is time to start singing again, for the promises for their future are also in the ground like a seed that is going to grow into a huge tree. It needs watering to come to life. As they begin to sing, the heavenly rain will come. It will be slow at first, as the parched soil drinks the rain, but slowly the ground will fill and the water will flow in strength as it floods across the land. It will be so great that it will wash away the demonic activity that has tried to keep my people captive. There will be people with repentant hearts forgiving and asking forgiveness and as their tears pool into rivers there will be an open heaven over the land. This spiritual rain infused with tears will make the tree of life grow greater than any tree ever seen in the natural. The tree will then explode into a holy fire that nothing will be able to quench, as long as they keep singing. At this time, they must be on their guard against misguiding lawmen and religious people who will come and try to sow confusion. These people are nothing but wolves dressed in sheep's clothing. If my people focus on the flame of the fire, they will see things clearly. It will burn brightly and begin to spread throughout

Nebo, Haasts Bluff, NT

the whole of Australia. People will come from all around the world to warm their hearts in the flame of this supernatural revival."

That is as much of the vision as I can reveal at present. In fact, I have edited the story for publication. I know this account may bewilder some people who are of the belief that if you can't touch something, it can't be real. It is just my story and it has taken courage to share it, as it opens me up to all kinds of opinions.

Sometimes we are afraid to share our hearts for fear of rejection but if you have a dream, why not dare to live it and share it.

I believe Australia has a great future ahead, but we need to see the "Paddles of Life" applied to our hearts to bring revival. It will begin in the spiritual realm before it manifests in the natural. For too long we have sat back and allowed our nation to be bound by fear.

Now we need to rise up and once again become a people of hope and faith.

The fire I speak of is already crackling in the heart of Australia. Because of their openness to the spiritual dimension, our indigenous people have a pivotal role. In one remote area, the indigenous people have been singing nearly every night for many years. They call this "Sing Along" and this is the singing my old friend Nebo spoke of. They are not singing to politicians or to dreamtime spirits; they are singing to the Creator of the universe. As the flame spreads, others are beginning to join in and spot fires are igniting across our nation.

I find this exciting and I want to be part of it, no matter how small my role may be. So who will join the faithful chorus and help usher in the glorious future our nation has in store?

On the road to Gundagai, NSW

Forgiveness is the fragrance that the violet sheds on the heel that has crushed it.

MARK TWAIN

Overcoming Fear

When I'm travelling in America, people who pick up on my accent often tell me they would love to come to Australia, but they believe we have too many dangerous animals. It's true we do have a few nasties, but they rarely bother you unless you do something silly. For example, if you swim in areas inhabited by saltwater crocodiles, you could have a problem. But if you take reasonable care, you'll be fine. Crocodiles don't venture far from water, they can only run fast in a straight line, and they don't climb trees. Not so the American grizzly bear! That animal is one keen, mean fighting machine. He can run faster than a horse, swim and climb trees. It seems the only thing he can't do is fly, which isn't much comfort, because neither can I!

I went with a friend to Denali National Park in Alaska to photograph Mount McKinley. In preparation for the trip, I tried to find out as much as possible about mountain biking, backpacking and camping out in bear country. The head ranger's briefing about grizzly bears went like something like this.

If you encounter a bear, try to ignore it. If it shows interest in you, look big. If it charges, stand still – it may be just a false charge (apparently bears like to play chicken!). If the bear keeps coming, roll up in a ball and play dead. I was thinking to myself I would probably pass out at that stage. There was a pregnant pause, so I asked, "Then what?" Mr Ranger answered, "Well, good luck. You'll have to fight back." What a fine thought – hand to hand combat with a grizzly bear. I know who I'd put my money on! Then the ranger regaled us with horror stories of people being mauled by bears – even dragged from their tents.

Fear can be healthy in certain situations – it prepares us for fight or flight. But nagging worries about marauding bears can be a waste of time and energy.

Over the years, I'd learned that preparation prevents desperation, so I went to a nearby outfitting store to speak with a local. I said we were going mountainbike riding in Denali National Park and asked what we would need for protection against bears. Straight up, the guy said, "You need a gun, a big hand gun." I said, "Listen, mate, I'm here to shoot your wildlife with a camera, not a gun. In Australia only the police and the criminals have guns." He laughed and suggested I try bear bells (a bit like sleigh bells on a bracelet) so we bought two sets each so we didn't accidentally surprise any grizzly bears. Later we found out that mainly tourists wear bear bells. Locals refer to them as "dinner bells" because they let the bears know dinner is on the way.

So we set off into the wilderness on our mountain bikes, jingling all the way, and rode down a steep hill to this stunning location, Wonder Lake. We were awestruck by the vista. How could anyone not believe in a creator?

It was summer in Denali. We would shoot the sunset, then, a couple of hours later, shoot sunrise. To top it off, there was a full moon this night, so the moon ran a relay race with the sun.

After taking heaps of photos, we went back to the bikes. Off in the distance we saw a large moose near a pond. I thought it could be a photo opportunity, but my friend was not convinced. As the moose started coming towards us, he took off up the hill on his bike. With one eye on the advancing moose, I quickly secured my camera gear to my bike rack, then started pedalling like I never had before.

Wonder Lake, Denali National Park, Alaska

The moose was charging right for me at the speed of a galloping horse, with headgear the size of a Mac truck bull-bar. My bike was in high gear from our earlier downhill run, but I am not a lycra-wearing, shaved-leg, professional bike rider who can pull off smooth gear changes under pressure. I decided I would just stay in high gear in case I messed up the change. With adrenaline pumping, I was moving fast up the hill. I thought I was going to rip the sprockets off those gears. I probably could have won the Tour de France that day. But still the moose was gaining. He was so close I could hear him snorting. Then, just as I was considering a high-speed turn back down the hill to try and dodge past him, the moose stopped. Phew!

As I got back to where my mate was waiting at the top of the hill – presumably so he could report back to my wife if I didn't make it – Mr Ranger came along and asked how we were going with the bears. "No problems with bears," I reported, "but I just got chased by a huge moose." When he said, quite matter of fact, "Far more people get killed by moose than by grizzly bears," I asked, "Then why didn't you warn us about moose?"

So the moral of this story is that we can spend an enormous amount of time and energy worrying about the bears in life, but often, in the end, you get charged by the giant moose!

The carnival, The Entrance, NSW

Some cause happiness wherever they go; others whenever they go.

OSCAR WILDE

The Carnival

The annual carnival at The Entrance over the Christmas holidays was a fun family activity that we all looked forward to. Great rides, shooting galleries and many other attractions, plus fantastic show food, like "Dagwood Dogs" – my favourite.

I knew the owners of the carnival and was aware of their battle with the local council as they strived to keep the annual carnival going. Many other pressures were also being placed on them by the politically correct – the ones I call the "take-away-all-fun-and-freedoms brigade".

On the last year the carnival was allowed in this area, I supported it by taking my entire extended family. The young ones wanted to go on a ride that would whirl you around at breathtaking speeds while you were locked in cages that also spin. You had to remove everything from your pockets or centrifugal force would do it for you. I knew the operator of the ride and he encouraged me to join the kids. Off we went. Before long, I didn't know up from down, or left from right. The operator thought he was doing me a big favour giving us a full-tilt ride. I was feeling really ill and the Dagwood Dog I had eaten was threatening to make a comeback. That would not be pretty in a caged area. I started waving desperately to get the operator to stop, but he thought I wanted more, so on and on it went. When it finally stopped and we emerged, the operator could see I wasn't doing well. I was as green as a tree frog. Apologetically, he said, "I just wanted to give you a ride to remember." He certainly did that.

Inside the big top, Lennon Bros Circus, Gosford, NSW

Taming the lions, Lennon Bros Circus, Gosford, NSW

The Circus comes to Town

As a child, I lived in a small country town. We didn't have a zoo like some big cities and although I had seen pictures of wild animals like elephants and lions, I never dreamed I would see them for real.

Then one day the circus came to town, with a gala parade down the main street to announce their arrival. There were clowns and jugglers – all kinds of people in different attire – plus lions and tigers prowling back and forth in their cages. Two huge elephants brought up the rear.

My friends and I were elated – our senses overwhelmed. As the elephants went past, one even left a present that any child would be thrilled by. My friends and I scooped it up in a big bin to take to school for Show and Tell. Surely our teacher would be impressed by this – it was the biggest poop we had ever seen. Unfortunately, our teacher wasn't at all impressed with our Show and Tell. But that didn't dampen my enthusiasm for the circus and its animals.

Many years later, when I was married with a beautiful little daughter of my own, the circus came to our town. The big top was up and all the animals were there. I could hardly wait to take my family to the circus. My family loved it and I could see the excitement and wonder in my daughter's eyes as she watched all the different acts.

I was so impressed by the show that I obtained the owner's permission to return and take some photos. As we were talking, the owner told me we were lucky to have had the circus there at all. Animal liberationists were trying to get councils to ban any circus with animal acts, because they believed it was cruel to the animals. As I spent time photographing the circus people, I discovered that they cared for their animals like family members. All the animals were in great condition.

There are laws in place to deal with people who mistreat animals and if it wasn't for the circus, there would be no life at all for those animals. I have photographed a lot of wild life since then, and life in the jungle is no picnic for animals either. I'm sure many animals would love a safe job in a good circus. I am proud that our local council didn't bow to the demands of the zealots, although apparently the vote was close. Wimpy councils all around Australia are banning circus shows with animals. I believe if these animals could speak, their question to the zealots and councillors would be: "Don't you want me to have a life at all?" I believe as much as anyone in protecting the rights of animals, but common sense must prevail. We should ensure animals are looked after, without taking their lives away. I don't understand why some people have to become fanatical and ban something that has been going on for hundreds of years.

Are we going to have to tell future generations that our politically-correct, over-regulated society killed the circus? How will children experience the excitement of seeing wild animals come to town? I will never forget my own excitement, nor the amazement on my daughter's face when the circus came to town. As a child I thought I took my teacher the biggest crap of all, but now I know there are bigger issues.

Raining on the rock, Uluru, NT

Hear my cry, O God; listen to my prayer.

From the ends of the earth I call to you, I call as my heart grows faint;

lead me to the rock that is higher than I.

For you have been my refuge, a strong tower against the foe.

I long to dwell in your tent forever and take refuge in the shelter of your wings.

PSALM 61:1–4 (NIV)

Anger or Angels

As I awaited sunrise that day on North Curl Curl Beach, I had no idea that one of my photographs would reveal in a wave the shape of a huge angel with its wings spread wide, plus three others looking on from below. It's harder to see this in the small image shown here, but in a print these features become obvious.

I had arrived well before dawn to get into position so no one could spoil my view. Generally, if people realise you were there first, and that you were set up waiting for a photo opportunity, they're very understanding and will work around you until you get the shot. I was all set up waiting for the sun to rise and to light the image I thought would be a winner. I was feeling good.

Suddenly a lady materialised, seemingly out of nowhere. She sat down right in the middle of my shot and began meditating. She had definitely seen me and must have realised what I was trying to do. But she just ignored me, closed her eyes and began to chant. I would love to say that I felt love for that woman, but my first reaction was annoyance. The only love I could muster at that precise moment was that I would have loved her to move.

There she sat, being one with the universe and tuning out everything around her. I called out to ask if she could move just a little to the side for a few minutes while I got my photo. Her only reply was to continue her incantation, "Om, Om, Om," which translated means "I am, I am, I am." I know this because I've meditated many times. I wasn't impressed. I was thinking, "I'm part of the universe too and you are, you are, you are in my shot." I was tempted to go over and tap her on the shoulder to get her attention, but I knew that would probably create a conflict situation. I realised I was angry and that is definitely not the time to start trying to get your own way. Often the cause of anger is simply that we're not getting things the way we think they should be. So I started to take it out on God. He has broad shoulders, plus He's always listening and knows what I am thinking, so I thought I might as well have my day in court.

"Hey God, in the Bible when Moses asked you what your name was you answered, 'I am the great I am.' Maybe this lady is trying to get through to you and you can tell her to move. Lord, this isn't fair – I was here first." And so on, as if God didn't know what was happening. When I finally ran out of puff, I felt as if God was saying

North Curl Curl Beach, NSW

to me, "Ken, just move." So I changed my position.

Within minutes, the sun peeked over the horizon and everything came together in divine timing for me to capture this picture. Through all my huffing and puffing, I'd come close to missing it. Initially I wanted to fight for my rights, but ultimately I praised God for the meditating woman. Maybe she was sent to help point me in a different direction?

If we're not careful, we may get everything our own way and miss the opportunity to be with angels.

*I saw the angel in the marble
and carved until I set him free.*
MICHELANGELO

Jim Jim Falls, Kakadu, NT

Peace like a river – how refreshing that stream,
That calms deep within us, like a wonderful dream.

PAM BONNER

Go with the Flow

People tend to think that clear, blue-sky days offer the best photo opportunities. While such conditions can sometimes produce good shots, often you end up with a lot of boring, predictable images. Some of the most dramatic photographic opportunities occur in wild, fluctuating weather. In conditions like that, you're forced to go with the flow.

You see, photography is a lot like life. You can be sailing along under clear skies with everything going fine, and you can be feeling nice and comfortable. Then a situation might arise that changes the game plan. Some people want to live their whole lives in that safe space. Well, if they're happy, that's fantastic; for me, though, it becomes boring and way too predictable. I personally like a bit of drama and stretching, which, I find, helps build character and also provides great stories and memories.

That's why landscape photography is so fulfilling. It gets you into the real world, where the rubber hits the road, or – in this case – where your feet slosh through freezing mud!

My assistant and I were trudging through rainforests in the northern New South Wales hinterland. The weather was cold and wet, which is actually perfect for shooting forests and waterfalls, but camping out in that stormy weather wasn't much fun. Occasionally we would take refuge in the local pub to thaw out a bit before continuing our adventure. One day, while we were warming ourselves in front of the pub's large open fireplace, a local came rushing in from outside and headed straight for the fire. "Oh man," he said, with a broad smile, "it's so cold out there, the dogs are sticking to the trees!" What a character – and what a word picture. We were laughing our heads off as we headed out into the cold again.

I believe we reveal our true nature and potential when we are under pressure, or outside our comfort zones. Sometimes our reactions aren't pretty, but if we're brave enough to honestly look at our responses to tough situations, over time we can learn not to be mastered by our emotions.

For over a week, my assistant and I endured that wild, rainy weather. We walked for miles and encountered leeches by the thousands. But what an adventure. I came away with many great shots from that area (see opposite, bottom).

Finally, we decided we had to find somewhere to dry out. We headed west over the Great Dividing Range until we found the sun and the sunflowers that we had hoped would be in flower. The weather here was a great improvement on our previous location. It was glorious to be in the sunshine again and we spent several days driving around the Gunnedah area looking for potential shots. On one special morning, we found a lovely field of flowers (opposite, top), but in the pre-dawn light I could see the wind moving all the heads. I knew if it didn't stop, the flowers would be blurry in my image. We decided to wait and our patience was rewarded as the morning unfolded. Just before the sun rose triumphantly, the light was magical and the wind just died. I was thrilled to be able to get this shot, which I have called "Let There be Joy". What a wonderful start to our day.

In life we have to endure many different conditions, but in each there are rewards. I find the key is to just go with the flow. Stormy seasons make the sunshine so much more special.

Sunflowers, Gunnedah, NSW

Dorrigo National Park, NSW

A Gift

The Stuart Highway runs from Port Augusta in South Australia to Darwin in the Northern Territory. For many locals, it's a lifeline running through the centre of Australia known simply as "The Track".

Small towns are sparsely scattered along this ribbon of highway and when asked for directions, the locals talk in terms of so many hundred kilometres up or down The Track. Its "centre" is simply where you happen to be at a particular time. It's not a very well-travelled road, although it's becoming busier with each passing year and in some places is barely wide enough for a truck and a car to pass. The unseasoned tourist is confronted with numerous hazards – both natural and manmade. Road trains probably present the greatest danger.

A road train is a large truck which hauls two or three trailers full of cattle, food supplies or other goods over huge distances in the outback. When one of these thundering juggernauts comes hurtling towards you at over 100 kilometres per hour, the wise driver gives it a wide birth. The trucks often drive in the middle of the road, to avoid having their wheels go off the bitumen. People who stick to the principle – admirable in theory – that all vehicles have equal rights on the road, are likely to end up decorating a road train's bull bar. "Might is right" is a far more appropriate dictum in this situation. It's a bit like the joke, "Where does a huge gorilla sit?" Wherever it wants to, of course.

My first trip up The Track was in 1980, when I was just beginning my photographic journey. I still had a lot of city slicker in me back then but I was off on a journey of discovery. In those days much of The Track was still dirt and even more perilous than it is today. It was while travelling along this road – dodging road trains and avoiding treacherous potholes, kangaroos and a variety of other wildlife – that I discovered an interesting custom of outback travellers. People invariably waved as they passed each other on the road which, with my city background, I found rather strange at first. If you waved at everyone you passed in city traffic, you would probably end up with a wrist strain injury. I think one reason for waving to strangers is the reassurance people feel at seeing another human being in the vastness of the Australian outback. They feel less alone; less vulnerable. It wasn't long before I began to enjoy the custom and waved happily to all who passed. It sometimes landed me in difficulties – like when I had to swerve in mid-wave to avoid an oncoming road train – and more than once I found myself sliding about precariously in loose gravel. But I was determined to share the love.

I found it disconcerting on the odd occasion when people didn't wave back. I made excuses for them – maybe she didn't see me wave; maybe his reflexes were a bit slow. But still, I felt slightly cheated when someone failed to return my wave. I pondered the reason for this irrational feeling and realised I wasn't waving simply to say hello, but because I wanted something in return.

This seemingly small insight has been of great benefit to me. It has helped me understand that we should give without expectation of a return. Greeting other people, even strangers, is an expression of affection. Love and affection should, like any gift, be given freely and unconditionally.

On the road to Oodnadatta, SA

THOUGHT

Our journey through life is not always easy. Yet the unexpected twists and turns can develop character. After all, straight roads may become monotonous and may trap us in the same boring ruts that many have travelled in before. We may wish for the easiest possible path, but every life has its trials and tribulations. We have to endure many different circumstances, but in each there are rewards. The key is to go with the flow. Diamonds are formed under extreme pressure, then ground and polished to sparkle. So, if you're under pressure, don't give up. Just hang in there – your days to shine will come.

The Pink Roadhouse, Oodnadatta, SA

*The Oodnadatta Track runs off "The Track". People in remote outback
Australia need to have a great sense of humour or they would go crazy.
Lyn decided, just for a laugh, she would paint everything in their business
her favourite colour: pink. And so was born "The Pink Roadhouse".*

Coles Bay, Tas

Getting out of Bed

In the late 1990s, I was invited to be a guest speaker for a photographic conference in Tasmania. It was held in a beautiful 5-star hotel at Coles Bay and attended by many inspiring professional photographers from all over Australia. I enjoyed meeting up with my fellow photographers, many of whom were good friends.

During my speech, I shared about many different aspects of my work, then finished with a question time to make sure I hadn't put them to sleep. Everyone was still rather spritely and questions came thick and fast. Someone asked the very pertinent question, "What's the hardest part of photography?" I quickly replied, "The hardest part of photography is getting out of bed. Lots of people have dreams and ideas, but they just need to stop procrastinating, get out of bed and get on with it."

During the lunch break, I noticed a wharf leading out from the hotel and thought perhaps it was worth a shot. That night everyone partied hard and many went to bed late. The next morning, I arose well before sunrise to capture the pre-dawn pastels painting the scene before me. What a wonderful way to start the day. As I was about to pack up, another photographer straggled on down to take some shots. He had missed the best light and asked me how it went. I told him I thought I might have a keeper. So, while most were still sleeping, I had been fortunate enough to capture a shot that has become very well known. When those who attended that conference see this shot, they remember me saying that the hardest part of photography – and life – is getting out of bed.

Lake Kambalda, WA

The Dividing Line

These reflections in a large salt lake evoke for me the concepts of earth and heaven. The fine white line of salt accentuates the dividing line between them. The interesting thing about this photo is that it breaks the commonly accepted "rule of thirds", which teaches that the best compositions in art generally position a subject one third of the way across – or up, or down – the page. When this photo was shown at an exhibition, it completely befuddled a visiting photography professor. Not knowing that I was the photographer when I came up to her, she burst out, "He's put the horizon in the middle! He's broken the rule of thirds. But it works!" Still not letting on who I was, I said, "Well, isn't it good the photographer didn't allow the rules to confine him." Of course, I'm well aware of these "rules" and often follow them, but I also know there are times when we should go beyond such self-imposed restrictions. In photography, as in life, keeping things simple can often bring peace and beauty to what we do.

For me, heaven and earth are part of the same journey. What is done on earth will be reflected upon in heaven. The creator has given us rules and guidelines – not to strangle us with religion, but to set us free. He wants us to fly high above our carnal nature and experience heaven on earth. Like salt, knowing right and wrong can stop things from going rotten. I believe the blueprint for right and wrong lies within us all. Which we choose to follow, will determine whether we see heaven reflected on earth.

New England, Vermont, USA

Divine Intervention

Like a patchwork of reflected colour, this scene from rural Vermont glows with the hues of autumn. Photographing it, however, proved quite a challenge.

My assistant and I discovered this location while travelling through Vermont. We tried to find the farmer who owned the property to ask permission to photograph it at sunrise, but when we couldn't locate the owner, we just hoped it would be okay.

We got up hours before sunrise and drove to the location in the dark, listening to a Christian radio station on the way. A preacher was droning on about how people should be more respectful to God and stop asking him for trivial things like parking spaces or help with the weather, because God is busy. I remember thinking to myself at the time, "Wow, he's talking about me. I'm constantly asking for God's help with all sorts of things."

We arrived at the farm well before sunrise and positioned ourselves beside this dam, hoping for some reflections. The wind was blowing, but the radio preacher's words were ringing in my ears. I thought, *I can't ask God for help; He's busy*. So we just set up the gear and waited.

Just then, a wild stallion approached us from the other side of the paddock. I told my assistant not to encourage it, but he had seen *Black Beauty* as a child and wanted to befriend this horse. Suddenly, the stallion reared up on its hind legs and tried to push me and my gear into the lake. Having been raised on a farm, I knew I had to show the horse we weren't afraid. So I shouted, "Whoa!" and gave him a hard slap on the head. That did the job; he left us alone. The

Jenne Farm, Vermont, USA

wind continued to blow and I waited, unwilling to ask for divine help.

Then along came Mrs Farmer, on her way to the barn. She saw us at the dam and shouted, "What are you doing in my paddock?" I called back that I was from Australia, travelling around taking photos for a book on America. I told her we had tried to find the property owner, but couldn't. "There's a wild stallion in this paddock!" she warned. "Yes," I replied, "we met him!" I assured her I knew all about horses… was virtually born in the saddle. So she said, very graciously, "Well, have fun! I have to go to town." And off she went.

About two hours passed and still the wind was blowing. My assistant, who wasn't a Christian, finally said, "Ken, why don't you ask God for help? He usually delivers." That got me thinking again. This time I started to think as a father: *If my daughter needed something, wouldn't I love to help her? And if I couldn't help her with small things, how would she be able to trust me on big issues?* Then I realised that God is the best father ever, so of course He loves to help me too. That poor preacher on the radio obviously had it wrong. He must have been baptised in lemon juice.

So I called out, "God, if you could please give us a hand and stop the wind so we can get a reflection on the water, that would be great." Guess what happened? The wind stopped immediately. My assistant said, "That took you long enough."

Now I'm not saying God is my personal set coordinator or lighting technician, but over the years He has helped me many times in so many ways. He is concerned about every aspect of our lives. You don't have to slap wild horses before you call.

It's Not about Us

The day before I was due to leave home to fly to Hawaii, my American assistant rang to say he'd broken his hand and wouldn't be able to accompany me. I considered waiting for him to recover, but because of the impending deadline for my first American book, I decided to go alone.

When I arrived in Hawaii, I went to see an old friend and his new partner who had invited me to stay with them. They lived right on the beach at Pipeline. True friendship is a wonderful thing. Though we hadn't seen each other for years, we picked up right where we left off, as though there had merely been a pause in the conversation. His new girlfriend was a lovely woman. But as we all talked, and though the conversation was pleasant, I sensed some tension in their home. Something was weighing heavily on their hearts, but I didn't know what.

Late that afternoon, feeling guilty about not taking photos, I went down to the nearby beach. Watching the glorious sunset, I recalled the day's conversations and pondered what had gone unspoken. It was then, I believe, God showed me the nature of this couple's problem.

Back at the house, I gently shared with them what I felt God had very specifically revealed to me on the beach. As I had just met this lady, I felt I should tread carefully. She listened to what I had to say, then ran from the room crying. My friend followed, trying to console her. I sat there thinking, "Gee, that went well. I have totally offended them on my first day here."

Soon the couple returned, somewhat composed. I apologised for telling them what I thought God had said and explained that I didn't mean to offend. My friend's girlfriend said, "Ken, what you said was exactly what I needed to hear. Our relationship has been pretty strained and I knew we needed help. I was told you were a Christian so, before you came, I vowed that if you told me certain things, I would believe God is real." The things I had said were a very precise answer to this lady's cry for help. Group hug and sighs of relief all round. Over the following days we had many deep discussions as I revealed how my faith in God is my source of peace and strength. So much for my book deadline; quality time with my friends was far more important.

During breaks in our conversations I would take photos from their roof, or wander on the beach to grab a few shots and recharge with God. After a few days of sharing together, my friends began to see what can happen when we hand over our problems and concerns to God. At first it was hard for them to relinquish control but as God ministered to them, His peace began to fill their hearts and they felt His miraculous love and healing power at work within them. To this day they are powering on.

My assistant's hand healed quickly and we both realised his absence was an opportunity for me to spend that quality time with my friends. I was also blessed by the time I spent with them, for if you're willing to help others along the way, God will look after the desires of your heart as well. God blessed me with more shots than I could have hoped for in my short strolls with Him along Pipeline beach.

Sunrise, Oahu, Hawaii

Sunset, Oahu, Hawaii

Pipeline, Oahu, Hawaii

Ultimately we know deeply that the other side of every fear is a freedom.

MARILYN FERGUSON

The Lone Cypress, Carmel, California, USA

That's Ridiculous

In this dreamy dawn shot, the Pacific Ocean plays at the coast's rocky feet while the famous Lone Cypress looks out upon the morning.

This tree is one of the landmarks of California's celebrated Monterey Peninsula. Countless tourists pause to view it as they make their way along the popular 17 Mile Drive. In fact, the Lone Cypress has become such an icon that the local Pebble Beach Company has even attempted to claim copyright over it, and great effort has gone into preserving it. This shot was taken before anyone tried to lay claim to it. It was just a humble little tree trying to hang in there.

Sometimes I feel I should produce a T-shirt that says "That's Ridiculous!" because there seems to be a great lack of common sense in the world today. And it seems to be getting worse.

I love America – the nation and its people. But, just like us here in Australia, they are losing too many freedoms. We're supposed to be part of the free world, but when people want to claim ownership of a tree, well, that's just ridiculous. Some ideas really should never see the light of day. How can people lay claim to creation? God – not humans – made trees. Creation should be for all to enjoy, not just for those who have money.

This tree's symbolism is profound: a solitary tree on the edge of a continent – one individual against the ravages of the world. The cypress is holding out against those who want to claim possession. Hang in there, brave tree! It's better to stand alone in freedom than to become a slave to the masses.

View from Hunts Mesa, Monument Valley, Arizona, USA

In God We Trust

When I get the feeling that an encounter with a particular person or place will result in future connection, I explain it as "unfinished business".

I feel that way about America. Even after publishing two books on the USA, I believe there's still more for me to do. It's not about business in the material sense; it's about spiritual business.

In 1838, Abraham Lincoln delivered a passionate speech in which he warned his nation of trouble ahead. He said: "At what point, then, is the approach of danger to be expected? I answer, if it ever reach us, it must spring up from amongst us. It cannot come from abroad. If destruction be our lot, we must be its author and finisher. As a nation of free men, we must live through all time, or die by suicide."

America is one of the most beautiful nations on earth. Why? I believe it's because God never wanted them to doubt that He is their strength. America is one of the greatest God-fearing nations in the world. Their currency proudly states, "In God we Trust," unlike many other nations where money *is* God. It's America's faith in God that will empower them to win back freedoms they've lost through fear. But it's that underlying faith in God that's under attack from within, as the enemy knows it's their strength.

In Monument Valley, I was overwhelmed by the spectacular display of God's handiwork. Yet I sensed the pain that America would have to go through and I started to weep. Then I was comforted as I felt God say to me, "Don't worry. My people will awaken."

The New Millennium

Sydney had won the bid to host the first Olympic Games of the new millennium. How exciting.

Some of my photographs had been used as part of the submission to secure the Olympic Games for Sydney. Then we were invited to supply official Sydney 2000 merchandise. The organisers wanted us to produce books and fine art prints that would embody the spirit of Sydney and Australia.

We felt honoured to be able to secure the rights to produce licensed products for the Sydney 2000 Games. Little did we know we were walking into a bureaucratic tornado. Nothing was simple or straightforward. Every decision required multiple approvals, convoluted legal documentation, thousands of regulations, reams of paperwork and more hurdles than any track event. It seemed to me like a case of political correctness gone mad! All the shots I'd taken of Sydney that had any brand name visible – other than the names of official Sydney 2000 Olympic Games sponsors – had to be subjected to massive digital manipulation to remove all branding. So I had the only sterilised book on Sydney I've seen since advertising became commonplace. People who saw my book must have thought Sydney was an ad-free zone. In stark contrast, the official sponsors had their logos plastered everywhere. They had more coverage than a big top over a flea circus.

Some years later, the organising committee for the Melbourne Commonwealth Games approached us. They had seen our Sydney Olympic Games merchandise and wanted us to produce similar products. We detailed our many bad experiences from the Sydney Olympics, but they assured us they would be much easier to work with. So we were sweet-talked into producing another book on Australia and a sponsor-friendly book on Melbourne.

For the Melbourne book, I wanted to shoot a game of Australian Rules football at the MCG and a Melbourne Cup race, both of which I felt were quintessential Melbourne. Try as I might, I could not obtain permission – not even for the Melbourne Commonwealth Games. I discovered that rights to photograph both events are owned by American photo libraries. How could we have allowed icons of Australian history to be owned by overseas companies?

Now I understand there are commercial realities to be considered, but I believe things have gotten a little out of hand, especially when it comes to photographing major events. No longer can professional photographers just turn up to capture images of important events to preserve for future generations. Photographers need to be accredited and certain organisations have been able to purchase exclusive rights for taking photos at these events. So their contracted photographers take the shots for their particular industry or interest, with no concern for preserving the atmosphere or history of that event for posterity. In this new millennium, I think we've lost something special from the past.

The highlight for me in photographing for all the official licensed products, was when was given special permission to shoot The Twelve Apostles from the beach. I spent days there waiting for the right light. Millennia come and go, but there was no need for a tornado of bureaucracy on that beach – just a great park ranger, a colony of friendly fairy penguins, and me. Now *that* gives me hope for the future.

New Year's Eve celebrations, Sydney, NSW

Opera House, Sydney, NSW

The Twelve Apostles, Vic

Shoot for the moon. Even if you miss, you'll land among the stars.

LES BROWN

Kimberley boabs, Derby, WA

Only God can make a tree – probably because it's so hard to figure out how to get the bark on.
WOODY ALLEN

I Still Call Australia Home

I was helping Qantas Airlines find locations for a new ad campaign. They wanted to film a large group of children singing "I Still Call Australia Home" in a variety of quintessential Australian locales. For one shot, the cinematographer wanted footage of boab trees in rich red dirt, with some indigenous children as well. I knew the perfect spot, so I flew to Derby.

All vegetation loves our rich, red, Aussie dirt (called Pindan soil). I knew that boab trees living in that type of soil would generally have an assortment of other flora crowded around them. Not wanting to destroy any vegetation, I decided to use some trees I knew about on the tidal floodplain near Derby airport. But the soil around those boab trees was grey. I needed help to get some red Pindan soil from a nearby quarry and spread it around the trees.

Hearing of our dilemma, the local mayor offered to lend me some of their big trucks and a front end loader, since it would be good promotion for the town of Derby. When I asked how much it would cost, the mayor replied, "A case of beer for the workers should do the trick."

I spent hours directing heavy equipment to create a scene I knew the cameraman and director would love. To top it off, I called my friends at the local indigenous community and they sent over a busload of their kids to join in what had become a great adventure.

The film crew and young singers flew straight into Derby Airport and were able to walk over to the set I'd created not far from the runway. The cinematographer could hardly believe I'd pulled it off. He said, "This is even better than I imagined. How much did all this cost?" When I told him it would cost him a new computer for the indigenous community and a case of beer for the workers, he threw his head back and laughed. Such is life in the Top End!

The Monastery of the Temptation, Mount of Temptation, Palestine

Over the Edge

An American publisher had contracted me to produce a book called *Where Jesus Walked*. While shooting, I was trying to raise funds to help finance the project, since the publisher's advance didn't cover all the travel and photography for the high-standard publication I wanted to create. My desire was to do this for the glory of God; I wanted it to be my best effort. I was trying to negotiate sponsorship deals with the Israeli Ministry of Tourism and some large companies – the same way I had raised capital for previous book projects. When I found it impossible to obtain financial support for the project, my wife and I decided to put everything on the line and finance the shortfall ourselves.

I wanted to get some shots at the Mount of Temptation in Jericho, where it's believed Jesus was tempted by Satan. My assistant and I arrived at the Palestinian border gate to find it had been closed. No one was allowed in.

The Israeli border guards said there were active terrorists in that area and there had apparently been threats that tourists would be taken hostage. It was very kind of them to be concerned for us, but I explained I had to get in there to shoot for a book deadline and offered to absolve them of responsibility for our safety. They wouldn't relent – I was locked out.

As we were reluctantly turning to leave, a taxi driver called out from the Palestinian side of the border and got our attention. We spoke to him through the fence and he said if we went about eight kilometres down the road we would come to a place where we could cross the border by running over a few sand dunes. He promised to meet us in the dunes in his yellow taxi. The guy seemed legitimate, and as this seemed like our only hope of gaining access to the location we decided to take up his offer. So we went for it.

Mount of Temptation, near Jericho, Palestine

I've never run so fast. The last thing we wanted was to be shot by border guards who might mistake us for terrorists. As we ran I realised what a huge gamble we were taking and I was very relieved when we saw that yellow taxi.

Because there were no tourists in Jericho, everything was very cheap, so we found a 5-star hotel to stay in. The next morning our newfound taxi driver friend drove us to our location, and we climbed up the mountain to the place where Jesus was tempted. While we waited for the right light, it began to rain. Then my wife called on my mobile phone. She told me there were problems back at home. Things were tough financially because of the money we were spending on this project. I assured her it would be okay, but when I got off the phone I felt disappointed with God. There I was doing a project I believed He wanted me to do, having to sneak across borders and getting rained on. Worst of all, I was missing my family, and my wife was having to deal with problems back home. I wasn't impressed so I called out to God and said, "We could lose everything on this project. We're totally over the edge." Just then it seemed I heard God speaking, asking simply, "Everything?" which really made me think. I said, "Well, everything besides you." Then it seemed God said to me: "Am I not enough? You have been trying to do things the way you have done before, but I will provide the finances for this project. You have been trying to do this project in your own strength." Instantly realising the truth of this, I just said, "Sorry, Lord; I'm certainly over the edge on this project, so I'm giving it back to you. I'll give it everything I have, but only you can make it happen."

Soon after that the rain stopped. Before me lay a view similar to one Jesus might have seen in His time of testing. Then a double rainbow appeared over the valley as a sign to me that all was well. I understood that God had everything under control and His peace returned in my heart. From that day on, God did supernaturally bless our business with finances and the project was completed. I thank God for meeting me over the edge – and all the praise for that project belongs to Him.

View from the Mount of Temptation, Jericho, Palestine

THOUGHT

People often tell me they like to live life on the edge.

I think if you're living on the edge, you're taking up space.

If you really want to live life to the max,

step over the edge of your own limitations and life will become very exciting.

Arts Freedom

It's been said that the state of the arts is a reflection of the state of a nation. If that's the case, then alarm bells should be sounding. Australia is in trouble. Photography in this country is under attack and photographers are losing the freedom to practise their craft. I find this particularly sad in light of the important role photography plays in capturing and preserving our history. Photography is able to immortalise moments in time more accurately and with greater realism than any other medium. When people think of Marilyn Monroe, they don't necessarily think of her films, but rather of the still photo of Marilyn with her dress blowing up.

In Australia, images by both professional and serious amateur photographers have been instrumental in defining our modern history. Photographers have faithfully catalogued and preserved their images for future generations.

When I started out as a photographer, there were very few restrictions or regulations if I wanted to photograph nature or people in public places. I went travelling around Australia with a dream to produce a book on my great nation. Never once was I pulled up by a government official and told I had to have permission or pay fees to take images. But today, if a young man wanted to follow in my footsteps and produce his own book on Australia, it would be rather different!

This is how it would unfold if he followed all the rules:

Let's say this young man decided to start by shooting Sydney Harbour or Sydney Opera House. He would need permission from either Sydney Harbour Foreshore Authority, Sydney Harbour National Park or Sydney Ports Corporation. After determining which authority governed the area he wanted to shoot from, he would have to advise which days he was coming. So he would have to be either a weather forecaster or a fortune teller to predict when the best light would be. Then he would have to unravel the applicable fee scales. If he survived all that, he might decide to shoot Bondi Beach. For that, he would have to ascertain which council manages that beach and apply for a permit. Again, he would have to advise which days he would be shooting, and pay their fee for a permit. For balance, he might want to shoot the northern beaches, so he might head for Manly where he would repeat the entire rigmarole.

If the young man hadn't given up by this time, he might go to the Blue Mountains to shoot The Three Sisters. That's a state run park, with different rules and yet another fee to pay for a permit. If he wanted to cover other NSW state parks and rang the relevant authority to find out what that entailed, he would be advised to buy an annual pass for around $200. But he would still have to give advance notice to each park he intended to visit. With hundreds of state parks in New South Wales it would take a lot of time and money to cover them all.

If anyone ever had enough time and energy to survive all this red tape and then dared to cross the border into Queensland, all I can say is: "Watch out." Queensland parks are even more regulated than the ones in New South Wales and each governing body has its own set of rules and regulations. I dare these over-zealous bureaucrats to do everything by the rules they have authored or allowed. I'm certain they'd never manage to produce a book on Australia.

So what happens to the young man who wants to do a book? Ultimately he might say: "Hang the rules! No one owns copyright on creation. If I require no more access and am creating no greater impact than the general public, I shouldn't be harassed."

Photographers' rally 2010, Sydney, NSW

Of course this line of thinking is common sense, but the young man will become a criminal if any of these governing bodies decide to take action against him.

I was very proud of my industry on this day in Sydney when photographers from all over Australia peacefully protested against the erosion of our rights and freedoms. Be warned politicians and bureaucrats; like the miners of the Eureka stockade, we have had enough. People will only take so much before they revolt against stupidity.

Don't get Stuck in a Box

Life is full of exciting possibilities and adventures if we're willing to change and grow. Unfortunately, we can often feel pressured to do things a certain way or behave the way others want us to. "Significant others" can even encourage us to stay the same, because that's what they're comfortable with. Perhaps we're fearful of how those people will react if we dare to seek change, so we compromise our dreams and live in limbo. But how would a bird know the joy of flying if it remained in the comfort of its nest?

We can box ourselves in through our relationships and associations. We all tend to have our particular groups of friends, social circles, professional organisations and recreational clubs – for some the list is quite long. Do these relationships enhance us or confine us? This is an important question. It can be difficult to see exactly where we are in life, until we look back from further up the road. Then we wonder what took us so long to get where we are.

It's much the same with photography. My photographic theme song could be "Should I stay or should I go?" by The Clash. Should I stick with the shot I set up for, even though it's not feeling magical? Or should I be willing to go after the shot that I can't yet see? As much as we might look to others for the answer to this question, it's up to each of us to learn how to hear the quiet voice trying to lead us.

Many people know me mainly as a panoramic photographer. But, while I'll always love panoramas, should I let that format be the only thing to define me? No – I don't want to be stuck in a box. I love photographing in many different formats: extra wide panos in 5:1 ratio, Lumix 16:9 ratio, Nikon 3:4 ratio, and my Phase One 3:4 ratio (see pictures on the following pages). I don't even want to be confined to two dimensional photography; I love 3-D as well. But most of all, I don't want to be defined as just a photographer, because I believe photography is merely a tool through which I can share my vision with others. My passion is to show the beauty of God's creation and my dreams go way beyond just taking photos, although I love capturing images along my journey. All the images I have taken so far have memories attached. Looking at a picture, I can be taken back to a particular time and place and remember what God was trying to show me at that time – or I remember if I missed the mark completely.

I believe God has a purpose and a destiny for each person. So for me, the key to life is finding His will for my life and having the courage to go for it. I'm still very much a work in progress; I've made many mistakes along the way. But gradually I'm learning to hear His voice more clearly and discern His will for me. With some trepidation, I say: "Bring it on, whatever the cost, and give me the strength to follow."

Should I stay or should I go? I have no choice but to go on, because I don't want to be held back when exciting change is in the air.

Cape Otway Lighthouse, Vic

When people ask what my favourite photo is, I tell them it's the next one.

KEN DUNCAN

Ormiston Gorge, NT

Finke River, West MacDonnell National Park, NT

Man's heart away from nature becomes hard.

CHIEF STANDING BEAR

Wildlife Love Affair

After capturing my now-famous image of an elephant in Zimbabwe, "The Power of One", I truly fell in love with shooting wildlife in medium format.

My main camera at the time was a Linhof 617 film camera with a very wide-angle lens; I needed to get very close to whatever animal I was photographing, which at times could be pretty dangerous. Even after being charged by that elephant, then later chased by lions in Tanzania, I stuck at it. The incident that finally forced me to reconsider my choice of camera was when three rhinos in Botswana wanted to play chicken with me. I knew I needed to get a medium format digital camera system so I could use longer lenses. Otherwise I wouldn't survive wildlife photography.

The Phase One digital camera I was already using for my landscape work seemed like the obvious choice. With its 80Mb sensor, it matched the resolution I was getting on my film camera. The only problem was that the Phase One didn't give me a long enough lens for shooting wildlife. Fortunately, I was able to get a very rare Mamiya 500mm f4.5 lens to fit the Phase One. That lens – equivalent to about a 300mm lens on a 35mm format camera – allowed me to bring the wildlife closer, without undue danger. The only obstacles were that it had no image stabilization and only allowed for manual focus and exposure.

I took my new toy on our next African photo safari, mounting my camera and lens on a sturdy tripod with gimbal head for maximum stabilisation. But I was surrounded by people using 35mm systems – plus my wife and daughter with their great Lumix cameras – all of which are far easier to use.

I had major problems focusing quickly enough and missed many shots. My highest ISO was 200, so my shutter speeds were low and I had to use mirror lock to stop mirror vibration on slower exposures. I was getting terribly frustrated. The last straw was when a leopard jumped out of a tree and my wife showed me the photo she'd snapped. She'd nailed the shot and her image was sharp, while I'd missed the magic moment because I couldn't respond quickly enough with all the different things I had to consider.

At that point I was ready to give up on the new gear and go with the flow like everyone else, shooting with smaller format cameras. I'd never heard of anyone pulling off what I was trying to do; I was sorely tempted to take the easy road.

As I brooded over my dilemma, I realised that often in life, when you try something different, it's really difficult. If it was easy, everyone would be doing it. I decided to push the frustration aside, steel myself and not give up. I had to persevere with my new gear and understand I would miss some of my shots. But when I managed to get it right, the resulting photos had the chance of being very special.

The reward for my tenacity was the photo on the following page. I had waited hours for this precise moment and while the file was opening on my computer I wondered how sharp it would be. When I zoomed right in on the image, I was overwhelmed by the clarity. I had nailed my first winner and the detail was almost mind-altering. So my wildlife adventure continues.

Leopard, Botswana

Elephant, Kenya

Lion, Botswana

Our deepest fear is not that we are inadequate.
Our deepest fear is that we are powerful beyond measure.

NELSON MANDELA

Gorillas, Rwanda

Zebra, Tanzania

THOUGHT

Life is a bit like a zebra: it has natural rules and regulations – areas of black and white.

Although we may dwell in shades of grey, I believe we each have an innate sense, like a voice inside, that tells us right from wrong.

We can choose to listen to the warnings of that inner voice, or allow ourselves to be overwhelmed by the noise of the world.

Victoria Falls, Zimbabwe

When the power of love overcomes the love of power, the world will know peace.

JIMI HENDRIX

Pasha Bulker stranded, Nobbys Beach, NSW

Stuff Happens

Early on the morning of 8 June 2007, the Newcastle Port Corporation radioed fifty-six ships off the coast that were waiting to load coal. The Corporation warned the carriers to move out to sea to escape an approaching storm. The *Pasha Bulker*, along with ten other ships, failed to heed the warning.

When the storm hit, *Pasha Bulker* was unable to clear the coast and ran aground on Nobbys Beach, Newcastle. The crew members were rescued in a daring and dangerous helicopter operation, but the vessel itself remained stranded thirty metres from shore. Its bow and stern were stuck firmly in the sand. Although empty of cargo, the ship carried around 700 tonnes of fuel, threatening a major ecological disaster if released.

A Danish company was awarded the contract to salvage *Pasha Bulker*. Their plan used anchors laid out to sea, which the ship would use to winch itself seawards with three tugboats towing it. Preparations to refloat the ship began on June 28, with ballast water being pumped out to aid buoyancy and tugboats pulling on lines attached to the bow. The vessel appeared to move for the first time, but an ocean swell of up to four metres pounded the ship and one of the cables snapped, dashing the attempt. Salvage efforts resumed the following morning, but were hampered by more cables snapping. Another attempt was made on July 1, when three salvage tugs managed to rotate the *Pasha Bulker* so it was facing deep water and only a few degrees short of clearing the reef. However, oil slicks were detected nearby so salvage operations were suspended amid concerns about a potential oil spill. It was a case of third time lucky when the ship was successfully towed off the reef on July 2.

In life, stuff happens. Rather than looking back and thinking "if only...", we need to just deal with it. The person in charge of the *Pasha Bulker* salvage operation had a plan and believed with all his heart he could refloat the ship. The media was all over the event and everyone had an opinion. Most people were sceptical the ship would ever get off the beach. Some specialists suggested the salvage company was just wasting time and the ship should be cut up where it stood. As each attempt failed, the doubters seemed to become more vocal.

I love the fact that the person with the vision to save *Pasha Bulker* never gave up. On the day he eventually succeeded, there was not a doubter to be found.

Dipsticks of the Outback

We are blessed to live in this beautiful country and it's hard for me to imagine how anyone travelling through outback Australia could fail to be inspired. Lately In my travels though, I'm starting to realise there's a strange breed of hooligan who feels the outback is theirs to trash. Rather than allowing the beauty of nature to wash over them, these people feel the need to leave their mark. Like feral cats staking out their territory, these people leave their names emblazoned on anything they can, as if they're mighty explorers who want to leave their names for posterity. "Hey look at me! I'm so intelligent I can write my name." I call these great thinkers "dipsticks" which (if you don't know) is a derogatory term used in Australian slang to describe someone who is not very bright at all. In fact, leaving their names is testimony to their stupidity.

My latest run-in with graffiti, courtesy of a guy who calls himself "Gaz", was in Alpine National Park in the high country of Victoria. This is the land of legends; home of the high country cattlemen and "The Man From Snowy River". It is an important part of our history. I was looking for new high country huts to photograph and found Howitt Hut. There, on the door, Gaz had spray-painted his name. I put Gaz right up there as the king of the dipsticks. What was he thinking? I then went to look at Millers Hut in the same region. Once again, Gaz had beaten me there. This time he'd really outdone himself; he'd used a chainsaw to write his name – in letters thirty centimetres high – on the old log walls of the hut. I could barely believe someone could be so insensitive. How could anyone think this was normal behaviour? I wondered how many beers Gaz needed before he came up with this dumb idea. Where were his friends, who should have told him that only a dipstick would do something as stupid as defacing a part of our Australian history? People like Gaz rarely travel alone; they usually like an audience.

Can you imagine inviting a guy like this to your home for dinner? While you're out in the kitchen preparing the meal, Gaz uses his chainsaw to carve his name into your walls, because he wants to be part of your history. Or perhaps, as a parting gesture, he paints his name on your front fence. I would be less than impressed if Gaz left his calling card anywhere in or on my home; he would certainly become history.

The saddest thing about all this is that Gaz is not alone. When I looked more closely, I saw that others had also used chainsaws on the old wood of the high country huts. There was Max and Alan, and a host of others. Shame on you, Gaz– and all the others like you! I hope someone who knows you reads this story and lets you know you've been officially entered in the dipsticks hall of fame. The rest of them are dumb enough to add their own names to it.

On a positive note, I appreciate the many beautiful people in the world who do the right thing. We all need to make sure we stand up to Gaz and his mates and give them a hand to see themselves – even if one of them is holding a chainsaw.

Millers Hut, Alpine National Park, Vic

Howitt Hut, Alpine National Park, Vic

Our Island Paradise

Everyone loves the word holiday. "Yes, please," I hear you cry, "I'll have one of those!"

One of my favourite sayings (and one we should all remember) is: "Never get so busy making a living that you forget to make a life." So, if you need a recharge, here are the most exotic locations I can suggest. These are my two all-time favourite, island-paradise locations: Whitsunday Island and Lizard Island.

On Whitsunday Island, Whitehaven Beach and Hill Inlet are spectacular holiday hotspots that are among the most beautiful places on earth. The sand at both these locations is almost pure silica, and in bright sunlight is such a radiant white that you definitely need sunglasses.

The walk down Whitehaven Beach to Hill Inlet at its western end looks deceptively short, but in fact the beach is over six kilometres long. On a clear day, the swimming is incomparable. Big waves are rarely a problem, as Whitsunday Island is protected from the Pacific Ocean by the Great Barrier Reef. One of the best ways to enjoy this location is onboard a yacht – then you get to stay after most visitors have left for the day (tours are mostly between about 10am and 4pm).

Should you opt for the long walk down Whitehaven Beach, you need to be mindful of the tide changes. Hill Inlet can really only be explored at low tide and you need to get across to the other side of the inlet to discover the best photo and exploration prospects. If you really want to impress your beloved – or someone whom you would like to become your beloved! – then this is the place to go.

To add a little variety to the mix, another great island getaway is Lizard Island, off the Queensland coast north of Cooktown. There are only two ways to get there – by air or by boat – but it's worth the effort. Lizard Island is endowed with stunning natural beauty and has some of the highest-rated diving spots in Australia.

The 5-star resort on Lizard Island is a wonderful place to stay – unless you're looking to meet people. This is a very intimate resort and guest numbers are limited. The accommodation is really for couples, or for people who enjoy their own company. Some families holiday there, but young children aren't encouraged as they might disturb the other guests. I happened to be there alone; just me and my cameras, suffering in luxury. My bed was so big I would change positions through the night just to work the springs. At dinner time, amidst flickering candles, I was surrounded by loving couples gazing into each other's eyes. When love is in the air you know conversation is going to be minimal. So I settled back and played solitaire while waiting for my food. I wondered why on earth I was there without my wife.

But I digress. Let's get back to the point – beaches. Lizard Island has some beauties. Some are so appealing they could be used as sets for a romantic movie. As I waited – often hours – for the right light, occasionally a couple would wander in, as if auditioning for a part.

We Australians are truly blessed to live in this inspiring land. Our spectacular home gives us great hope for the future. There's nothing quite like a beautiful beach to help soothe the human spirit.

Hill Inlet, Whitsunday Island, Qld

Sunset Beach, Lizard Island, Qld

Russell Falls, Mount Field National Park, Tas

Faith is like a river; its momentum has the power to move through mountains.

KEN DUNCAN

Letter to a Rich Man

This is a story about a very well-known Australian; you will probably guess who I'm talking about as you read the details.

Some years ago, this highly successful businessman suffered a massive heart attack while playing sport. The only thing that saved him was the fact that ambulance officers, who had a defibrillator at the event, were able to shock his heart back to life.

The event received major media coverage. When the man was later interviewed, his famous quote went something like this: "I've been to the other side and there's nothing there."

As a landscape photographer I spend many hours waiting for the right light or weather conditions. During those times I often have what I call conversations with God. I just speak out what I am thinking; it passes the time and can even be fun. I don't always get answers, but some days it can be quite interesting.

One particular day, I was pondering what this businessman had said in his interview. Clearly he was a very intelligent person, otherwise he would never have been able to build the empire he had. As a Christian, I believe there's something on the other side of death, as do many people of other faiths and beliefs. I believe that our spirit is eternal – our bodies are just fertilizer for earth. In my younger years, I had a young friend die in my arms. While trying to save him, I had felt his spirit leave his body, never to return.

Remembering my young friend's death, I spoke out and said, "God, that businessman is no idiot. Am I deluding myself believing in heaven?" All at once it seemed God was answering me; I suddenly understood why there was nothing on the other side for that businessman. It was like this: If a man's savings were in the Commonwealth Bank and he went to Westpac and tried to withdraw his money, they would say to him, "Sorry, sir, but there is nothing here for you, as you don't bank at this place." So it was for the businessman. He was banking in the world and its system. Seemingly, he had no heavenly account set up; he didn't believe in anything beyond the earth. It wasn't the way God would have wanted it, but everyone has free will. Then I also had the distinct impression that God wasn't finished with that man yet, which is why he was still on earth.

I was very excited by these insights and felt I should send a letter to this man who had no faith in anything on the other side. Through friends, I made contact with the man's personal assistant, who knew of my work. I asked if it would be all right to send something in that could be important to her boss and she said it would be fine.

So I wrote down what I'd felt God had shown me and mailed it with a signed copy of one of my books. As I posted it I wondered if I was stupid to be sending a message to such a powerful man – it might upset him. But then I thought perhaps God was using me to get through to the man. Some weeks later, the businessman was gracious enough to reply. His letter basically said, "Thank you for your thoughts. They were interesting, but we'll have to agree to disagree."

I don't know what God did with all of that, but I believe I did what I needed to do.

Ethereal light

Laughter is the Best Medicine

What a blast it was to be invited onto this set to take special panoramic stills for the movie *Charlie and Boots*. I loved the movie, and I think over time it could become an Aussie classic. Beautifully shot and directed, the film really captures the quintessential character of Australians, and our wonderful rural lifestyle.

It was a pleasure to work with the movie's team. There were no precious princes or princesses – everyone just worked together like a well-oiled machine. Paul Hogan and Shane Jacobson have to be two of Australia's funniest men and I found it a real pleasure to be in their company. Like fire and oxygen, they'd feed off each other – you couldn't help but laugh. These are two guys I definitely wouldn't want to attend a funeral with, as I think we'd end up getting kicked out.

It is said that laughter is the best medicine. If that's the case, I reckon after working with these blokes, I could probably have climbed Mount Everest. They both told so many jokes and I tried to remember them all, but that's definitely not my gift. In the end, however, I did remember one joke that Paul told:

"Two nuns were driving along an outback road, when Satan landed menacingly on the bonnet of their moving car. They were both shocked, but the nun who was driving recovered first and shouted to the other nun, "Quick, show him your cross." When her passenger didn't move, she screamed louder, "Show him your cross." So the other nun carefully wound down the passenger side window, stuck her head out and screamed at the top of her voice, "Get off the bloody bonnet of our car."

Shane Jacobson and Paul Hogan on location, *Charlie and Boots* movie, 2009

You have to stay in shape. My grandmother, she started walking five miles a day when she was sixty. She's ninety-seven today and we don't know where on earth she is.

ROBIN WILLIAMS

Global Warming

For over forty years I've been closely observing creation and the state of the environment; it's my job and also my passion. In 2008 I had the pleasure of photographing Mawson's Huts in Antarctica. On my birthday, I was in the huts and saw the remnants of the old dark-room of one of my photographic heroes, Frank Hurley, who had been there 100 years earlier. I took photos outside from similar angles that Hurley had shot in his day, at the same time of year.

Later, during the peak of all the talk about global warming and rising sea levels, I looked at the two sets of photos, taken 100 years apart. There was more ice evident in my recent photos; if anything, the sea level was lower, not higher, than in Hurley's shots.

Personally, I'm fed up with people using the fear of global warming to try and bring in new laws under the guise of environmental protection. Protecting the environment is essential, but this whole thing is not about guarding the environment – it's about establishing a new international governing body under the Copenhagen Treaty. The authority of that governing body will take precedence over the laws of any country that signs the Copenhagen Treaty and it will have power of enforcement on whatever is deemed an environmental issue. I suspect too that a lot of funding from our carbon tax or an ETS will end up flowing to this new international power.

Power mongers try to frighten us, because people cowered in fear can be manipulated. They swamp us with excessive information we don't have time to read or analyse because we're busy trying to make a living and bring up our families. Even politicians don't read all the paperwork that comes across their desks. They get "executive briefs" which are very short, provide only the bare bones of legislation and don't highlight the loss of freedoms often contained in treaties and laws. I made it my business to read all 200 pages of the Copenhagen Treaty and I don't believe it's the solution to our environmental problems; all it will do is lock us up in taxing carbon emissions.

None of the climate change prophets of doom are dealing with the elephants in the room, one of which is our dependence on fossil fuels. Why? Because a great deal of money and power is involved. We all know there are other power solutions available, but our leaders won't take on the big players. I have read reams of documentation on climate change and I know the enemy is in the detail. I even spoke with the then Opposition leader, Malcolm Turnbull, encouraging him to stand up to the Prime Minister, Kevin Rudd. This was when Labor was threatening an election if the Liberals didn't vote in favour of the Emissions Trading Scheme. I told him the Australian people didn't want a carbon tax, but he argued that they did. I said, "Malcolm you're wrong and you'll lose your job," and he did.

Around that time an Australian company bought a lot of my work to decorate their offices, so I went to thank them. I asked what sort of work they did and was told they were into fusion energy. Wow, the holy grail of energy. I was impressed. I asked how long it would take to happen and the director told me they were already doing it and could run a city if they were allowed. "So what's the downside?" I asked. "Are there detrimental by-products?" He told me the only by-product is helium exhaust. So I asked what fuel they used for their fusion process and he replied, "We use deuterium which comes from the ocean and there's plenty to supply all earth's power needs for many generations. I can show you it working downstairs."

This ground-breaking Australian technology produces no harmful emissions – neither carbon dioxide nor any other greenhouse

Mawsons Huts, Antarctica

gases – so there's no carbon emission problem. How could this be? "With all the talk of carbon tax," I asked, "why isn't our government all over this new technology?" The director said, "Ken, they don't want to deal with the carbon issues; they want to milk the fossil fuel industry and give those companies time to move their finances into new technologies. I was almost speechless. "What about the Greens?" I finally asked. "They're the worst of all," he replied. "The climate change fear campaign is a vote winner for them." I later spoke to an independent nuclear physicist who had been brought in from the USA to test and verify their processes. I asked him if it was for real and he assured me it was. "This is revolutionary," he said. "It solves all carbon emission issues."

Why does the Australian public know nothing about this technology? Why, when I ask politicians what they know about this or other possible solutions (which I'm sure exist), do their eyes just seem to glaze over?

We're a smart country. Here's our chance to lead the way when it comes to pollution control. Let's not be run by lobby groups with fat cheque books. Let's demand a government with enough spine to tackle the real issues rather than sending all our pollution to China and other developing countries.

Penguins, Macquarie Island

LIFE'S A JOURNEY   131

Patagonia Paradise

One particularly enjoyable aspect of my job is taking groups of passionate photographers on photo expeditions to some of the world's greatest locations. My friend, Ray Martin, came along on this Patagonia adventure. He loves photography and wanted to learn more about it. Ray was a pleasure to have on the expedition. I love the way he keeps things simple, just shooting with his Lumix camera. He was very excited, running all over the place and getting great shots. I nicknamed him "The Energizer Bunny". He was more interested in catching magical moments than getting caught up in technicalities. Because he was constantly exploring, Ray managed to get more angles than anyone else. He'd come to learn from me, but in the end I told him he should just keep shooting his own way. He has a natural eye for a great photo.

After camping out overnight, we had an amazing morning photographing Mount Fitz Roy reflected in glacial lakes, before beginning our long descent to El Chalten. Suddenly we came upon this beautiful alpine meadow with a vibrant show of autumn foliage. I had difficulty deciding where to shoot from to convey the majesty of the scene. Meanwhile, Ray was talking with some fellow Aussies who had recognised him from his famous television appearances and were excited to meet him in the wilderness of Argentina. The light was changing with the varying cloud cover, but in this divine moment everything came together perfectly. The different layers in the image lead in to the towering peak of Mount Fitz Roy in the background.

I dedicate this shot to Ray, because, while he was being the nice guy, I got the shot that my Energizer Bunny mate missed.

Autumn, Patagonia, Argentina

Glaciar Perito Moreno, Argentina

The global warming scaremongering has its justification in the fact that it is something that generates funds.

EDUARDO TONNI, PALEONTOLOGIST

Committee for Scientific Research, Argentina

Photography Should be Fun

On our first African Photo Safari, my camera gear was large and cumbersome. However one of the people on our trip, Brian Peters, had a Lumix, which was a camera I'd never seen before. It was very compact, but had a great zoom lens made by Leica, who I knew made great optics. I was doubtful such a small camera could take serious images, but was really impressed when I saw the results. While many others were struggling with more complicated gear, Brian was having fun – shooting his head off and nailing heaps of great images.

Not long after that African trip I was a guest speaker at a photographic trade show. As I was passing the Panasonic stand, I saw the Lumix range and realised Panasonic were the manufacturers of these intriguing little techno-wonders. I went over to encourage them. I told them how impressed I was with the images I'd seen from one of their cameras. They knew of my photography and thanked me for the compliment. Then they asked me if I'd like to try out a Lumix myself.

So I had a lot of fun perusing the wonderful range of cameras they had on display at the show. I wanted something that was small but could shoot in RAW format. I chose the Lumix LX series of cameras. To this day it's a range I love. They're amazingly compact, which means I can always carry one with me for quick, candid shots.

I name all my cameras, and after I'd been shooting with this camera for a while I called it "Ridiculous". I was extremely impressed with how easy it was to use – and with the quality of the final images – so I'd often find myself saying: "It's ridiculous this little camera can produce such high quality photos!"

Previously, on special occasions, I would quite often pull my big camera gear out to take some family happy snaps, but it would take a long time. I remember one Christmas morning, my young daughter said, "Dad, enough with the photos! Let's get into the presents." My family's much happier now I have my Lumix cameras; family photos are fun again. The mantra of many photographers is, "Just one more please." But with "Ridiculous" you can capture special moments quickly and unobtrusively.

I still love my medium format, high-end professional equipment as I'm always after the highest quality images possible for my fine art prints (which are printed very big and therefore need the extra file size). My Lumix cameras just add another string to my bow. Cameras like this have really put a lot of fun back into photography. The quality is so good I've even used them for publications and magazine articles.

The picture alongside here is a fun shot that was made easy with my Lumix camera. I needed a classic Australian lifestyle image for a promotion, so I called my very creative friend Sheridan and asked if she would help. She agreed and even produced a swimsuit with an Aussie flag on it. So we went down to a local beach; as she frolicked in the sea, I was able to get this quick snap which is great quality.

I love the fact that modern technology makes taking photos easier. You still have to learn to see the picture, compose the image and capture the right moment, but other than that, you just snap away and enjoy your day!

Sheridyn, Bateau Bay, NSW

THOUGHT

As a photographer, it's important not to live your life through your viewfinder.
Sometimes you need to simply enjoy moments for yourself
without feeling the need to capture images for others.
In this respect, photography is a bit like life:
don't just be a spectator, be a participator – that's where the fun is.

Long Jetty, Central Coast, NSW

Toowoon Bay, Central Coast, NSW

The sun is up, the sky is blue,
it's beautiful, and so are you.
THE BEATLES

The Art of Photography

Back in the early 1980s, photography wasn't really considered an art form in Australia. However, I believed photography was worthy of full art status, and that it deserved its own high quality art market. Just as with painting, the art of photography is in seeing the image; the craft is the way you capture and present it.

I only started my own galleries because no one was taking the sale of photographic art seriously. I felt I had to try and do it myself to prove there was a market for photographic art. If I succeeded, hopefully other photographers could join me in making a living by shooting what they loved, rather than having to take commercial assignments.

Years on, photography is now one of the fastest growing art forms in the world – especially with the younger generation. The art world has also woken up to the *collectability* of photography with many new galleries and exhibitions opening. The inception and rapid growth of the internet has also helped fine art photography go from strength to strength.

Aspiring photographers often come into our galleries to investigate how we present our work. They're usually easy to recognise; they're the ones who want to look really closely at the prints. When I see someone doing that, I usually ask if he or she is a photographer. If the answer is yes, I then ask, "Would you also like to be able to sell your work one day?" Almost always, the answer is yes. Next I ask, "So whose photographs have you collected?" Quite often, the young hopeful will admit he or she has never bought another artist's work. So I gently say, "As a photographer you need to know what's good, what's collectable. How will you ever convince others about the collectability of photography, if you don't have anyone else's work?" I don't say this so they'll buy my work, but hopefully so they'll develop an appreciation for the art of photography.

Many painters are also collectors who buy or swap works along their journey. They're passionate about the art world, not just about their own work. Many famous painters have left behind fantastic collections of paintings from a variety of artists, because they've recognised what was good.

Photographers need to think like this as well, and develop a passion for the art of photography. One of the biggest mistakes I ever made was letting a friend talk me out of buying an Ansell Adams print back in the 1980s for a couple of thousand dollars. That print today is worth over $US500,000 and is still appreciating in value.

Photography is an art form, and as much as I love taking photos, I'm also a collector. When I see a great shot, I can appreciate it without feeling the need to replicate it. If I love it and can afford it, I'll buy it. Or I'll try to swap prints with the artist. Too many photographers are imitators rather than creators; they go out and try to copy images that others have made famous. That's okay for those just starting out, but at some stage they should try the road less travelled and see what they can create. You can go and shoot Bridal Veil Falls in Yosemite National Park just like Ansell Adams – your shot may even be technically better – but the Ansell Adams image is the money shot. Why? Because it was taken and signed by him.

Aerial, King Sound, The Kimberley, WA

HOW TO PRESENT A FINE ART PRINT

Over the years I have learned that quality is paramount in the display of fine art photographic prints. We print with Epson Ultrachrome pigment-based inks on Hahnemühle White Ultra Smooth Photo Rag 100% Cotton, 305gsm. Each print is sprayed three times with Hahnemühle UV matt varnish. We mount on Gatorfoam mounting board, with Neschen Gudy 802 water-based, double-sided adhesive film and use museum quality mat boards and 4.5mm Shinkolite® Acrylic. For the highest quality and most elegant result, we use Bellini Fine Mouldings.

LIFE'S A JOURNEY 141

Taj Mahal, India

Chasing Tigers

My desire to photograph tigers led me to Bandhavgarh National Park in India. Photographers there for *National Geographic* were amazed at my medium format camera and said I would never get close enough with that sort of gear.

After three days in the park, I hadn't captured a tiger shot I was happy with, but I hadn't lost hope. On our last game drive in the park, my driver suggested we take one last look for the young tigers and I readily agreed.

We reached the area that he thought would provide the best opportunity. There were cars everywhere. Everyone was trying to get a shot of tigers in the grass, but they weren't in a good position. My driver said we should move up a bit and wait, as the tigers might come to us. So we left everyone else to fight over average shots and went to take our "last stand". After we positioned ourselves, the mahouts (rangers riding elephants) stopped the other vehicles from following. They wanted to leave an exit route for the tigers if they did head our way.

Miraculously, three young tigers came and posed on a rock ledge right in front of me. The lens I had was ideal; all three cubs just fitted into my frame. From behind I could hear others yelling at us to move so they could shoot from our position, but the mahouts wouldn't allow any cars to move. All three cubs looked right at me, before disappearing into the forest. The *National Geographic* guys finally came up and said, "Don't tell us you just got the shot!" I said, "I think I did. And the gear I had was perfect."

Curious tiger cubs, Bandhavgarh National Park, India

Imagine all the people living life in peace.
You may say I'm a dreamer, but I'm not the only one.
I hope someday you'll join us, and the world will live as one.
JOHN LENNON

World Vision: Mother & Child

It's been a great privilege to work with World Vision over the years. They're one of the world's greatest aid organisations and I hate to think what a void would be left if such groups couldn't continue their important work around the globe. One of the keys to fulfilment in life, I believe, is to use your gifts and talents to benefit those who need a hand up. That's why I choose to get involved. Helping others gives me a profound sense of fulfilment because I'm making a difference – and it reminds me how blessed I am to live in Australia.

In 2010, I visited India with a team of World Vision artists. The plan was to let the artists meet the people World Vision serves, in the hope they would return and help spread awareness of the important work being done. We were a colourful, creative team – photographers, musicians, singers and even a poet. The plan worked; every person on the team was impacted by that trip.

Our trip coincided with the Commonwealth Games in New Delhi and the attendant media obsession with how many gold medals each country was winning. But it didn't take long for our group to see beyond the veil of going for gold. We visited projects in some of India's poorest areas. It was heartbreaking in one sense, yet uplifting, as we witnessed World Vision staff and volunteers bringing help and hope to people who had previously known only abject poverty.

The projects were many and varied: from education, nutrition and medical aid, to equipping people with employment skills. One issue that really hit me hard was child slavery. India has over two million children in forced labour and when we visited some children who had been sold into slavery, my heart broke. I believe these children are India's greatest potential for gold and we must take action to restore their freedom.

When we hear on the nightly news about tragic events like flood or famine, we're touched. But for the people directly affected, such events turn their world upside down and bring utter devastation upon whole families. Parents can be forced to make heartbreaking decisions just to give some of their children a chance for survival. If a family has four children, the parents may have the choice to place one child into forced labour so they can buy food for the rest, or let them all die. It seems impossible to us, but these are their only choices.

How can such inequity be allowed to continue? People are literally starving to death while billions of dollars are spent competing for gold. I really appreciate organisations like World Vision who are there to support those in need. Imagine the help and healing they could bring if they had the same funding as just one Olympic or Commonwealth Games event.

World Vision and I decided the best way I could help was by publishing a book. *Vision of Hope – Mother & Child* celebrates the universal bond between child and mother, and illustrates how small steps can become giant leaps. It highlights what's already been done and prompts us to imagine what more can be achieved. Proceeds from the sale of each book will help World Vision further support the needs of mothers and children in the world's poorest communities. Each child is gold in God's eyes and deserves every chance for the best possible future. By partnering with World Vision you can be part of bringing a Vision of Hope to millions.

A young boy polishes gemstones in Jaipur, India. World Vision is working with communities to help put an end to child labour.

LIFE'S A JOURNEY

Eight-year-old Dulamsuren from Bayankhongor, Mongolia, with her familiy's goat

Simplicity is the ultimate sophistication.

LEONARDO DA VINCI

Mother and child attending a mothers' nutrition and self-help group in Jaipur, India

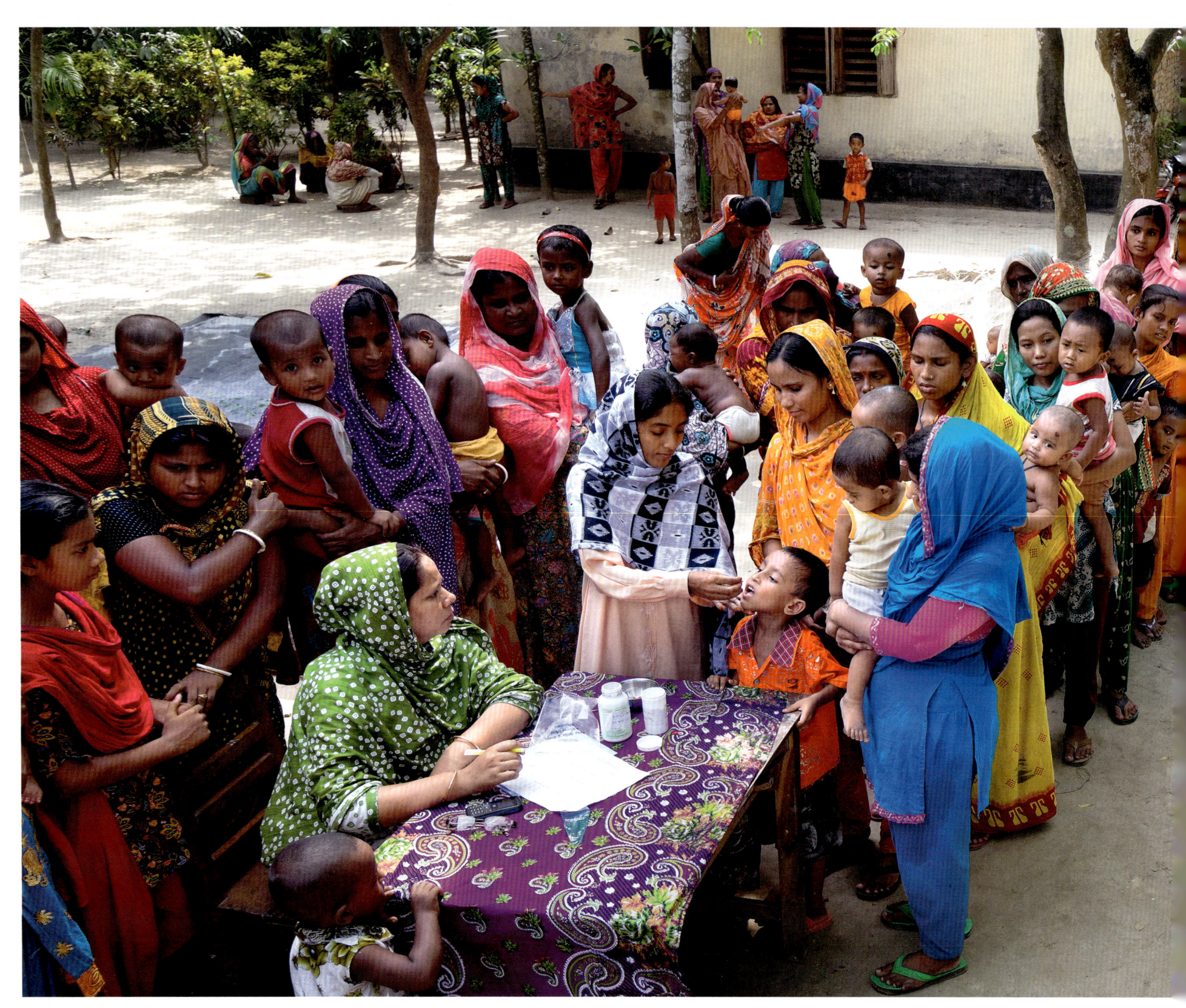

In the fight against global poverty, vaccinations can protect children against life-threatening yet preventable diseases.
Here, over 200 Bangladeshi mothers have brought their children to a World Vision supported immunisation centre.

LIFE'S A JOURNEY 149

Midnight Oil, Lake Lefroy, Kambalda, WA

Petrol bowser, Silverton, NSW

Essential Oils

Midnight Oil, in my opinion, is one of the greatest rock bands Australia has ever produced. They're all extremely passionate people and I feel privileged to have worked with the band and their management over the years. I never aspired to photograph rock bands, but I loved working with the Oils because they had something to say through their music. One of Rob's great lines still lives on strong: "The rich get richer and the poor get the picture."

Their music practically blew walls down; if you ever saw them live, you would know what I mean. Even if dancing didn't come naturally to you, the beat and the volume would've moved you. It saddened me when the new music stopped, and I still hope they'll start song-writing again. If ever we needed stirring themes and words of hope, the time is now (and I'm sure they all still have more to say). But whether or not they perform again, the songs they've already produced will live on and I'm honoured to have had one of my photos chosen for the cover of their latest album, *Essential Oils*.

As well as being talented musicians, they are a generous bunch of people with a real heart to help our indigenous people in outback Australia. When I asked for their help, they agreed without hesitation to personally sign a few prints of their *Essential Oils* cover artwork to raise money for the Walk a While Foundation.

Thanks Guys for all the great memories.

Midnight Oil on location, South Coast, NSW

LIFE'S A JOURNEY 153

Shining Light: New Zealand

People from all over the world have asked when I'm going to shoot more photos of New Zealand. I've always answered by saying: "It's a big world and no individual photographer can cover it all." Then I say: "I believe Andy Apse is one of New Zealand's finest photographers. You should buy *his* work. Andy's doing a fantastic job in New Zealand, so I'm leaving it to him!"

New Zealand *is* spectacular. It would be an exciting place to shoot in depth – but Australia and a select group of other countries have had my attention until now.

However, when I was asked to lead a photo expedition to New Zealand, I finally gave in – on the condition that Andy Apse came with us as our guide. No one knows that country better. Andy liked the idea, so we set off on an adventure in the South Island of New Zealand.

I looked forward to introducing my friends to Andy; I knew they'd learn a great deal from him. I also looked forward to spending time with him. There's nothing better than travelling and photographing together to really get to know a person.

On that trip, we all learned a lot about landscape photography from Andy. But I gained other valuable insights too. Andy has a great operation in New Zealand. His small gallery is attached to his home and all his books are produced through one outside publisher. His website is a platform for the sale of prints and image usages. He doesn't want to publish his own books or have lots of galleries; he wants to keep things simple. He put it like this: "Ken, it's all about lifestyle for me. I could grow my business and employ more staff, but I don't need those hassles. My wife and I handle everything with just one casual worker and that's all we need. I want to be free to do the things I love – hunting, fishing, exploring and spending time with my family. People need to phone before visiting my gallery, as I mightn't be there!"

Andy's simple attitude to life really impacted me. My wife and I have very full schedules, twenty staff, and many facets to our business. After listening to Andy, we began to think back on the beginnings of our business. Things were so much simpler in those days. We didn't sell anywhere near the volume of work we do now, but we had time to follow our dreams. Had we gotten off track somehow?

I think it's healthy to frequently examine where you are and where you're heading, to ensure you're not being driven. What fuels our consumer-driven society is people's desire for more. When is enough, enough? Some so-called experts claim that if a business isn't growing, it's dying. Is there anything wrong with finding a level you're satisfied with? I don't think so. There are more important things in life than worldly success. Lifestyle, family, friends – time for the things you enjoy doing – these are life's greatest treasures; they create the best memories. Regret is futile, but I think it's important to learn from the past so we can make better choices for the future.

Late one afternoon on our New Zealand adventure, I was granted this shot which really spoke to me. When we take time to really examine our lives, we often see more clearly the light that's shining on the landscape ahead.

Nevis Valley, New Zealand

Jade Dragon River, Guilin, China

China Awakens

China awakens – and with upwards of 1.3 billion people, that's a lot of breakfasts!

I've been amazed to watch the growth and development of China over recent years. The country and its people fascinate me, and it seems as though nothing on earth can stop their progress. I feel very drawn to the Chinese nation and am looking forward to future visits.

Admittedly, I'm not too keen on spending much time in the rapidly expanding cities; they're like giant whirlpools sucking people in from the rural areas. Many of the industrialised centres also have massive pollution problems, exacerbated by other countries not dealing with their own carbon emissions. I really don't think that sending all our production to developing nations, then blaming them for carbon emissions and leaving them to cope with the resulting health problems, is the way to save our planet. Hopefully, rather than playing the carbon trading game, China will turn this situation around and tackle the fossil fuel issue head on. If they do, they could become a world leader in environmentally friendly energy. Wouldn't that give the so-called developed nations a wakeup call.

Not for me the crowded cities. I'm more interested in continuing my exploration of China's natural treasures. There are many little-known gems, like Tiger Leaping Gorge on the Yangtze River; or Jiuzhaigou, with its bright crystalline lakes, snow-capped mountains and waterfalls. Adventure beckons in scenic Guilin on the Li River, with its craggy, mist-shrouded peaks and its fishermen working on bamboo rafts while tourists play on similar craft. The Chinese people love getting out into their national parks and with the size of their population, they don't need tourists to create a crowd. In fact, in many of these places international tourists are few and far between. My attractive daughter with her long legs and light brown hair was constantly asked to pose for photos and do the scissor fingers with the locals. She loved China. For her the only drawback was that she really wanted to buy a pair of the colourful locally-made shoes, but the largest size was thirty-nine.

I'm encouraged by the fact that the Chinese people have a love for their natural environment. Its beauty helps bring a sense of hope and peace, especially to those who have been caught up in the vortex of city life. In a nation growing as rapidly as China, the people need to be protective of their natural assets, lest they lose them. Balance is found when humanity works together with nature. If we don't respect creation, our actions may return to hit us on the head, like a boomerang.

Interestingly, as a professional landscape photographer, I felt more freedom in China, in some respects, than in my own country. Never once was I bailed up by an official and asked if I had a permit. They were just excited that I was enjoying their country. In contrast, in many areas of Australia, professional photographers are often treated like criminals. It made me pause and wonder which is the free country.

My hope for China is that they don't lose sight of who they are in their rush to embrace western culture. They have a wonderfully rich heritage and it would be sad to see them exchange it for the glittery baubles of the developed world.

I wish you the best, China. You no longer need to be imitators; it's time for you to shine with your own innate creativity.

Fisherman, Lijiang River, Guilin, China

LIFE'S A JOURNEY

Walk a While

An indigenous elder I greatly respect once gave me a precious key to understanding people: "If you really want to know someone," he said, "you need to walk a while with them."

We tend to look to government to bring about unity and reconciliation, but that only increases the likelihood of the process becoming polarised and more bureaucratic. I'm pleased our politicians have offered a national apology for the injustices our indigenous people suffered in the past, but politics won't bring unity to our nation. Unity will only be brought about by people who demonstrate and drive reconciliation. We'd all do well to learn to walk a while together in this beautiful country we call home.

About ten years ago, during a visit to Haasts Bluff, I realised that the people of the Ikuntji community – especially the youth – had little access to the technology most of us take for granted in the arts world. I felt I could do something to help. So we launched an initiative we call Walk a While to walk alongside the indigenous people of central Australia, using the creative arts as common ground. Our objective is to provide indigenous youth in remote communities with equipment and skills to empower them to tell their stories.

Initially Walk a While focused on photography, video and music. With some of Australia's finest artists working with us, the project has gained momentum. An important part of the plan is to show our indigenous friends how we make a living from our arts, so they begin to see wider choices for their future. This will free them from the cycle of government aid, which erodes their self-respect.

Until now, we've been taking our own equipment when we visit. But when we leave, so does our gear, and still the people have no permanent access to the technology they need. Our present goal is to secure a permanent building for the first Arts Centre, to house instructors and equipment. This will provide a base for training in a variety of technology-based creative arts, including photography, cinematography, music, website development and design.

We have people ready to man the centre and generous suppliers prepared to donate equipment and software. The Walk a While Foundation, now listed on the Australian Register of Cultural Organisations, is able to receive tax-deductible donations to assist in establishing and running the centre. Having already received donations from various individuals and corporations, we're now ready to take Walk a While to the next level.

Walk a While has the full support of the people of Haasts Bluff and the surrounding communities. They believe the Arts Centre will supply resources, training and encouragement to artists from all around the area. Walk a While will also work in cooperation with the local school, giving them greater access to the latest technology.

We are seeking government assistance to find a building and are extremely thankful for the support of the Honourable Alison Anderson, MLA, and her chief adviser, Kelvin McCann. They understand the world of government and are committed to helping us secure a base. We've identified certain buildings within the community that currently don't appear to be fully utilised, so we're drawing closer to our goal of a permanent base. Hopefully, by the time you read this we'll already have it. Every great dream needs a solid foundation from which to grow. So please keep us in your prayers and come "walk a while" with us.

Young budding photographers, Ormiston Gorge, NT

Revival in the Heartland

Since 1982, something has been happening in the heart of Australia. Almost every night, a group of indigenous Christians has been singing songs to Jesus for hours at a time. The phenomenon is known as "sing along". It hasn't been imposed on them by any other race; it's their own form of worship. I've visited many holy places and attended services of different faiths, but I've never experienced anything as powerful as sing along. When this singing starts, the heavens open and time seems to stand still.

Friends of mine from Haasts Bluff, Alison and Douglas, told me the singers were gathering at Easter at a place called Memory (near their community). Memory is the site of a monument in honour of the four indigenous evangelists who originally spread the gospel through central Australia. Tribes would be coming from all around to be part of this Easter sing along event in celebration of their Christian heritage. Alison and Douglas asked if I would come and bring some Christian musicians to join them. I quickly offered to bring some friends plus a generator and a PA.

I asked Pastor Brian Houston if he would send a small worship team from Hillsong. He was keen for his people to be involved. Pastor Wayne Alcorn from Brisbane City Church also agreed to send a team. My Pastors, Barry and Lyn, were right behind it too and sent a team of helpers, plus a harp player. My good mate, country singer Steve Grace, came as well.

Our eclectic band of musicians and helpers flew to Alice Springs then drove to Memory, where we joined hundreds of indigenous people from surrounding communities. In the shadow of Memory Mountain, on our red dirt stage under thousands of stars, the powerful singing continued for five consecutive nights. We didn't need a smoke machine; the dust did the job. Night by night the excitement mounted as black and white musicians mingled and played together. With harp sounds wafting through the air, the divine resonance of sing along opened the heavens above. I thought surely angels were coming to get us.

During that event, Alison, Douglas and Janet (another community leader) shared with me their vision to build a cross on top of Memory Mountain and asked if I would help. I said I'd be glad to (thinking at the time that probably a couple of bags of cement and a few planks would do the trick) as long as the indigenous communities helped too. I returned home and didn't give the matter much thought until I was visited by a friend, Graeme, who's an engineer. He asked what I had been up to and I told him about the concert in central Australia and my indigenous mates' desire to build a cross. Instantly, he said, "Can I help? I'll pay my own expense to come out and see what needs to be done."

Five years on, we finally have permits in place to build that cross. It will actually be twenty metres high, with solar powered lights, so it can be seen from afar. Many indigenous artists are providing paintings to help raise funds for the project. Alison has produced a painting called "Holy Spirit Fire" (see opposite) which is the story of the cross.

I look forward to the celebration when my friends' vision comes to pass.

Holy Spirit Fire

This painting depicts a vision that my people have about a cross being raised on our land at a place called Roundhouse Mountain (also known as Memory Mountain). We believe as this cross is raised up, proclaiming Jesus Christ over our land and our nation, it will help to ignite a great move of the Holy Spirit across Australia. For us, the raising of the cross will signify to all spiritual powers and principalities that we are covered by the blood of Jesus and that He is our strength in the spiritual battle we face. When it is erected, the cross will draw people to it. We believe as people come together in unity, focussed on the Cross of Jesus Christ and the victory it represents, we will see a mighty move of the Holy Spirit. It will be like a fire burning in the heart of our nation and spreading throughout the country.

Alison Multa, July 2013

West Macdonnell Ranges, NT

I lift up my eyes to the mountains – where does my help come from?
My help comes from the Lord, the Maker of heaven and earth.

PSALM 121:1–2 (NIV)

Index of images

Aerial, King Sound, The Kimberley, WA	141
Aerial, Lawn Hill, Qld	44–45
Alaska, USA	65
Albert Hotel, Burketown, Qld	48
Alpine National Park, Vic	40-41,119
Antarctica	129
Argentina	132–133, 134–135
Arizona, USA	91
Autumn, Patagonia, Argentina	132–133
Bandhavgarh National Park, India	143
Bangladesh	148–149
Bateau Bay, NSW	137
Bayankhongor, Mongolia	146
Benambra, Vic	42
Boabs, WA	96–97
Botswana	109, 111
Brighton Beach huts, Vic	10
Brumbies at dawn, Benambra, Vic	42
Bungle Bungles, Purnululu National Park, WA	52
Burketown, Qld	48
Burra Homestead, SA	27
California, USA	90
Cameron Highlands, Malaysia	56–57
Cape Leveque, WA	32
Cape Otway Lighthouse, Vic	105
Carmel, California, USA	90
Carnival, The Entrance, NSW	66–67
Central Coast, NSW	4–5, 66–67, 68, 137, 138, 139
Charlie and Boots movie, 2009	126–127
Chengdu, China	6
Chile	8–9
China	6, 156, 158–159
Circus, Gosford, NSW	68
Coles Bay, Tas	82
Curious tiger cubs, Bandhavgarh National Park, India	143
Daisy, Violet, Ken and Djomery, Derby, WA	19
Denali National Park, Alaska, USA	65
Derby, WA	19, 96–97
Dorrigo National Park, NSW	77
Dulamsuren, Bayankhongor, Mongolia	146
Duncan, James, on horseback, Kunmunya, WA	15
Duncan, Ken	13, 19, 59, 168
Duncan, Neta	17
Eight-year-old Dulamsuren with goat, Bayankhongor, Mongolia	146
Elephant, Kenya	110
Entrance, The, NSW	66–67
Ethereal light	125
Falls Creek, Vic	42
Farmer harvesting, NSW	29
Farmer Mel (Gibson)	34–35, 37, 38
Farmer's daughter, Wentworth, NSW	25
Finke River, West MacDonnell National Park, NT	107
Fisherman, Lijiang River, Guilin, China	158-159
Fisherman, Penang, Malaysia	59
Gemstones, Jaipur, India	145
Giant Panda, Chengdu, China	6
Gibson, Mel	34–35, 37, 38, 39
Glaciar Perito Moreno, Argentina	134–135
Glenrowan, Vic	22
Goat, Bayankhongor, Mongolia	146
Gorillas, Rwanda	112
Gosford, NSW	68
Great Barrier Reef, Qld	53
Guilin, China	156, 158-159
Gundagai, NSW	62–63
Gunnedah, NSW	77
Haasts Bluff, NT	61, 163
Harvesting, NSW	29
Hawaii, USA	87, 88–89
Hill Inlet, Whitsunday Island, Qld	Front cover, 54–55, 121
Hogan, Paul	126–127
"Holy Spirit Fire" by Alison Multa, Haasts Bluff, NT	163
Howitt Hut, Alpine National Park, Vic	119
Hunts Mesa, Monument Valley, Arizona, USA	91
Immunisation centre, Bangladesh	148–149
India	142, 143, 145, 147
Inside the big top, Lennon Bros Circus, Gosford, NSW	68
In the yards, Korumburra, Vic	25
Jacobson, Shane	126–127
Jade Dragon River, Guilin, China	156
Jaipur, India	145, 147
James Duncan on horseback, Kunmunya, WA	15
Jenne Farm, Vermont, USA	85
Jericho, Palestine	98, 99, 100–101
Jim Jim Falls, Kakadu, NT	74–75
Kakadu, NT	74–75
Kambalda, WA	83, 150
Kelly homestead ruins, Glenrowan, Vic	22
Ken Duncan	13, 19, 59, 168
Ken on top of Memory Mountain where the cross will be built	168
Ken with former Malaysian PM Dr Mahathir Mohamad	59
Kenya	110
Kimberley, The, WA	15, 16, 17, 19, 20–21, 28, 32, 52, 96–97, 141
Kimberley boabs, Derby, WA	96–97
Kimberley coast, WA	16
Kimberley kids, Cape Leveque, WA	32
King Sound, The Kimberley, WA	141
Koolewong, NSW	4–5
Korumburra, Vic	24, 25
Kunmunya, WA	15, 17
Lake Kambalda, WA	83
Lake Lefroy, Kambalda, WA	150
Lawn Hill, Qld	44–45
Lawn Hill Creek, Qld	47
Lawn Hill Gorge, Lawn Hill National Park, Qld	47
Lennon Bros Circus, Gosford, NSW	68
Leopard, Botswana	109
Lijiang River, Guilin, China	158-159
Lion, Botswana	111
Lions	68, 111
Lions, Gosford, NSW	68
Lizard Island, Qld	121

Lone Cypress, The, Carmel, California, USA	90	Ormiston Gorge, NT	106, 161	Taj Mahal, India	142
Long Jetty, Central Coast, NSW	138			Taming the lions, Lennon Bros Circus, Gosford, NSW	68
		Paddle steamer on the Murray River, Vic	23	Tangambalanga, Vic	34–35
Macquarie Island	130–131	Palestine	98, 99, 100–101	Tanzania	113
Mahathir Mohamad, Dr, Malaysia	59	Panda, Chengdu, China	6	Taylor, Robert	39
Malaysia	56–57, 59	*Pasha Bulker*, Nobbys Beach, NSW	116, 117	Tiger cubs, India	143
Mawsons Huts, Antarctica	129	*Pasha Bulker* stranded, Nobbys Beach, NSW	116	Toowoon Bay, Central Coast, NSW	139
Mel at political rally, Wodonga, Vic	39	Patagonia, Argentina	132–133, 134–135	Torres Del Paine National Park, Chile	8–9
Mel Gibson	34–35, 37, 38, 39	Pearling lugger, Kimberley coast, WA	16	Tribesmen, Kunmunya, WA	15
Mel Gibson, Tangambalanga, Vic	34–35, 37, 38	Penang, Malaysia	59	Twelve Apostles, The, Vic	94–95
Mel supporting independent candidate Robert Taylor	39	Penguins, Macquarie Island	130–131		
Midnight Oil	150, 152–153	Petrol bowser, Silverton, NSW	151	Uluru, NT	1, 70–71, Back cover
Midnight Oil, Lake Lefroy, Kambalda, WA	150	Photographers' rally 2010, Sydney, NSW	103	USA	65, 84, 85, 87, 88–89, 90, 91
Midnight Oil on location, South Coast, NSW	152–153	Pink Roadhouse, The, Oodnadatta, SA	80–81		
Millers Hut, Alpine National Park, Vic	119	Pipeline, Oahu, Hawaii	88–89	Vaccinations, immunisation centre, Bangladesh	148–149
Mitchell Falls, WA	20–21	Purnululu National Park, WA	52	Vermont, USA	84, 85
Monastery of the Temptation, The,				Victoria Falls, Zimbabwe	114–115
Mount of Temptation, Palestine	98	Raining on the rock, Uluru, NT	70–71	View from Hunts Mesa, Monument Valley,	
Mongolia	146	Reconciliation in action, Kunmunya, WA	17	Arizona, USA	91
Monument Valley, Arizona, USA	91	Red centre, Uluru, NT	Back cover	View from the Mount of Temptation, Jericho,	
Mother and child, Jaipur, India	147	Refuge beach, Vic	51	Palestine	100–101
Mount Field National Park, Tas	122–123	Refuge Cove, Vic	50, 51		
Mount of Temptation, near Jericho, Palestine	98, 99, 100–101	Reggies Hut, Burra, SA	27	Watt Leggatt pearling lugger, Kimberley coast, WA	16
Multa, Alison, Haasts Bluff, NT	163	Russell Falls, Mount Field National Park, Tas	122–123	Wentworth, NSW	25
Murray River, Vic	23	Rwanda	112	West MacDonnell National Park, NT	107, 164–165
				West MacDonell Ranges, NT	107, 164–165
Nebo, Haasts Bluff, NT	61	Shane Jacobson and Paul Hogan on location,		Whitsunday Island, Qld	Front cover, 54–55, 121
Neta Duncan, WA	17	*Charlie and Boots* movie, 2009	126–127	Wodonga, Vic	39
Nevis Valley, New Zealand	155	Sheathers Wharf, Koolewong, NSW	4–5	Wonder Lake, Denali National Park, Alaska	65
New England, Vermont, USA	84, 85	Sheep muster, Korumburra, Vic	24, 25	World Vision supported immunisation centre,	
New Year's Eve celebrations, Sydney, NSW	93	Sheridyn, Bateau Bay, NSW	137	Bangladesh	148–149
New Zealand	155	Silverton, NSW	151		
Nobbys Beach, NSW	116, 117	Sliding rock, Yirrkala, NT	33	Yirrkala, NT	33
North Curl Curl Beach, NSW	72–73	Snowy gums, Alpine National Park, Vic	40–41	Young boy polishing gemstones, Jaipur, India	145
		South Coast, NSW	152–153	Young budding photographers, Ormiston Gorge, NT	161
Oahu, Hawaii, USA	87, 88–89	Stockman's hut, Falls Creek, Vic	42		
Old Halls Creek, WA	28	Sugarcane fire, Qld	30–31	Zebra, Tanzania	113
Old Halls Creek Post Office, WA	28	Sunflowers, Gunnedah, NSW	77	Zimbabwe	114–115
On the road to Gundagai, NSW	62–63	Sunrise, Oahu, Hawaii, USA	87		
On the road to Oodnadatta, SA	79	Sunset, Oahu, Hawaii	87		
Oodnadatta, SA	79, 80–81	Sunset Beach, Lizard Island, Qld	121		
Opera House, Sydney, NSW	93	Sydney, NSW	72–73, 93, 103		

KEN DUNCAN
Life's a Journey
First published 2013
by Panographs Publishing Pty Ltd
ABN 21 050 235 606
PO Box 3015, Wamberal,
NSW, 2260, Australia
Telephone +61 2 4367 6777
Email: panos@kenduncan.com
This endition produced 2014
for Books & Gifts Direct.

©2013, Panographs Publishing Pty Ltd
This publication is copyright. Other than for the purposes of and subject to the conditions prescribed under the Copyright Act 1968 (Commonwealth of Australia), no part of it in any form or by any means (electronic, mechanical, microcopying, photocopying, recording or otherwise) may be reproduced, stored in a retrieval system or transmitted without prior written permission of Panographs Publishing Pty Ltd.
Panographs is a registered trademark of the Ken Duncan Group Pty Limited.

Photography & text by Ken Duncan
©2013 Divine Guidance P/L
Editing by Peter Friend
Design by Peter Morley,
Good Catch Design
Reprographics by CFL Print Studio,
www.createdforlife.com
Printed in China by Everbest Printing Co. Ltd.

The National Library of Australia Cataloguing-in-Publication entry
Author   Duncan, Ken, author, illustrator
Title   Ken Duncan: life's a journey / Ken Duncan
ISBN   9780987295859 (hardback)
Notes   Includes index
Subjects Duncan, Ken
          Photographers-Australia
Dewey Number 770.2

To view the range of Ken Duncan fine art prints plus books and other products visit:
www.kenduncan.com

Ken on top of Memory Mountain where the cross will be built

PHOTO BY WAYNE OSBORNE